Forever Scarred

The Unauthorized John Wayne Bobbitt Story
By
Christopher Mark Kudela

This is an unauthorized biography of certain events in the life of John Wayne Bobbitt, based on the statements directly made to the author by Mr. Bobbitt in numerous face to face interviews. The author has made every effort to accurately document those statements and has relied upon their factual correctness. However, this book is not sponsored, endorsed by, or approved of in any way by John Wayne Bobbitt or any other person or entity associated with him.

This book is dedicated to Christopher 'Bubba' Bennion.
May you forever rest in peace my brother.

Forward

This is the story of what really caused the most infamous non-death criminal case in United States history. I spent the better part of a year interviewing John Wayne Bobbitt. The following is the true account of what I was told by the man himself.

We were introduced when my first novel, 'They Call Me Krud,' caught some local attention and raised a few eyebrows. Locally it sold a few copies and surprised folks with the candor from which I spoke. One of 'John's people' had read it and suggested to him the possibility of contacting me for a chance to write his story. Turns out he had several authors that attempted to work with him only to all eventually concede defeat as he is literally exhausting on so many levels.

I live by a simple credo… always do your best in all that you do. I am happiest when in my creative element of writing. My mind, heart and soul pour from within me to sometimes enlighten, other times comfort, but always attempting to entertain. If you have something that you're passionate about, then dedicate yourself 100%, allow the others of the world all of the mediocrity they desire, as for me, I choose to shine. I want to be the best at what I do. This is the mentality that I bring to any project that I undertake, and this one would be no different.

This crazy roller coaster of a ride began one night as I was oblivious to what began to form around me. I was sitting at my editor's house discussing a project, when I received an email from one of John's people suggesting this book opportunity.

John's life was, is, and forever shall be riddled with status clinger parasites looking to suck off any flash of attention that he can possibly muster for profit. I called the number that was listed and after a few minutes of chatter we agreed to meet a few days later. The person who set the meeting was soon replaced by another inconsequential person, followed by another, and yet another. The influx of new faces would become exhausting and ultimately detrimental.

After agreeing to sign on board we would meet once, sometimes twice a week for grueling interview sessions. I explained to him this one simple philosophy, people are inherently good and want to forgive others. So, if he told the truth whilst offering an apology, he would ultimately be forgiven by the masses. Isn't that what we all so desperately crave, to be forgiven? I know I did, thus the reason that I began to write in the first place.

I had my first interview sessions in a group setting that included John, his brother Brett, my editor Dawn, and myself. I remember that I immediately felt as if I had bargained with the devil for my ticket to climb aboard this crazy train. Everything about it was repulsive. Because Brett had witnessed several traumatic events personally, by the second meeting John openly admitted to raping Lorena.

Brett just said, "Bro how are you going to lie right to my face after you know I saw you? You know it, and I know it, so just fucking admit it."

John eventually conceded and admitted to forcing Lorena to have sex multiple times during their marriage. To say it was a bombshell to me would be a bold faced lie, because I already knew that he did. What it did to the project on the other hand was devastating.

With my newfound wisdom of his crimes, I immediately began to write from my notes the book that you will soon be reading verbatim. I brought the first chunk of finished words to the team, and we had a discussion on where the project should go. To my surprise John considered it date night and there was a new face at our meeting. I knew from jump-street that this vacuous creature would be the downfall of our project together.

I said in front of everyone, "Really John, we're bringing strange new women to work to discuss how you repeatedly raped your wife. Wow... she's going to love this!"

Apparently her vagina trumped any rational thought in John's head. I banned her from all future meetings, but she managed to infect the ultimate decision of the project. That is all of the press I would like to give this person because she's truly one woman that I wish to forget.

Initially John had agreed to pay his brother Brett 10% of his own personal royalties, but as soon as he read the first portion of the book he pulled me aside, "I don't want to keep Brett on the book because I don't want to have to pay him. He doesn't deserve any of my money."

I instantly saw the greed in John's eyes and the shallowness of his soul. Brett was callously discarded by John's never ending quest for financial gain. I didn't like it but it was John's decision regarding his money, and truthfully, I learned years ago… NEVER get between two brothers.

The next explosion in the project came when Dawn decided she wanted nothing to do with the disgusting content of this book. Dawn is a consummate professional, a Christian, a mother, a Sunday school teacher, and above all… a wholesome, kindhearted, human being. Not only did the content shock and appall her, it sickened her to the point that she just walked away from the project wanting nothing for all of the work she had put in.

So there we stood, John and I, with a few measly chapters completed. We needed an editor, a story, basically a whole book. Brett was furiously screaming, Dawn wasn't speaking, and me… well, I was alone with John.

After a few weeks of interviews with John, as luck would have it, an old acquaintance Christie reached out to me for something entirely unrelated. Since she was brilliant, beautiful, and scholarly, I asked her if she wanted to climb aboard the crazy train of the John Bobbitt express. She agreed and off we went.

A publisher showed interest and after talks John and I agreed to sign with him. So with a new editor, publisher, and opportunity, we hit the ground running. This time around, our interviews were more intense and longer. We had a publisher waiting for a finished product and I was on a mission to provide him with one as soon as possible.

I will not lie, in all honesty I despised John as a person. But something peculiar began to happen. The longer that we worked together on the project, and the more he began to divulge, the more I began to feel for him. This didn't happen overnight mind you, this took maybe six or eight months to unfold and I'll tell you what cinched the deal. When he divulged that he was sexually assaulted in The Nevada Department of Corrections, I couldn't help but feel for him (but you will read all about that later). That was the literal explosion on this project. I had to call the publisher and let John tell him because it was so huge. John's concerns about being viewed as a homosexual with this admission were alleviated after a long conference call between the three of us. We signed a few papers to the validity of John's admissions, and I immersed myself whole hog into the project for another month until the book was completely finished.

It is and was exactly as I finished it. This 'Forward' is new, but all other portions are the same. John and I went over this same book that you are about to read and signed off on both the cover and interior proofs for the publisher to print.

John said, "It's the best book ever!"

The publisher loved it, John loved it, the editor loved it, and together we were all excited. After a year of listening to all of the depravity, interviewing a forever scarred, tortured and tormented soul the writing was finally ready for press. The publisher sent over a few proof copies and John took one home for his girlfriend to see. Well this is where it all spiraled out of control.

After her reading, said strumpet was none too happy. "We'll have to move out of the country if you release this book."

Those were her exact words. May I die a thousand torturous deaths if I am lying. She infected the entire flow of publication with her toxicity. From here on out it was, "Fuck you Chris! We don't like the way the book makes John look like a rapist."

To which I replied to both, "John you are a rapist. You admitted it. What about all of the papers that you signed?"

And this was John Wayne Bobbitt's response, "I lied under oath before and they believed me, I'll just do it again!"

The original publisher heard him say this, Dawn heard him say this, and I heard him say this. Nothing but hate filled death threats followed. John said he would kill me if this book ever reached the light of day.

The original publisher pulled out of the project because he said, "Chris, I can't be involved if I know that something could happen to you because of a book that I publish."

So I shopped it around without changing a word and got all of my ducks in a row. And though there are many who get thanked in the final section of the book, my most heartfelt is this, I would like to thank Jonathan Brown and the law firm of Lipsitz Green Scime Cambria LLP.

This 'Forward' has been added, but the rest remains the same complete with John's signed statements to the validity of his admissions. Enjoy...

Prequel

Domestic violence is a dirty and disgusting crime that has touched many lives in the United States of America. So many in fact, that it has touched mine. That is the reason that I have agreed to undertake this project, because my first recognizable memory is of domestic violence.

Picture me as a child playing on the linoleum floor of our modest kitchen. I was five years old and my mother was at the sink doing dishes when my father, without warning, abruptly barged in. He stormed across the room and grabbed her by the hair with murderous intent. In a lightening flash, he spun her around viciously and punched her in the face. She flew violently across the room and landed on the floor in a daze. Then, my father snatched her up and proceeded to drag her limp, semi-conscious body to the front door by her hair. Her screams fell on deaf ears as he picked her up and threw her outside. Simultaneously, I attacked him and struck him in the leg with the wooden rolling pin that I had been playing with. My father callously back-handed me, and I was sent spiraling across the room. I landed in a disheveled heap, discombobulated by both the impact of the wall, and my father's fist. I laid helplessly as my father ran back into the kitchen to grab my mother's keys. He returned with harsh words, threw the keys outside, and slammed the door. That was the last time I saw my mother until I was 13 years old.

I have seen domestic abuse firsthand, and hence, I have learned that if you are not part of the solution, then you my friend, are part of the problem. So I decided to use my passion for prose as a vehicle to bring this issue to the forefront of social consciousness. In order to do this, as the author, I knew that I needed to tackle this subject head on. I would need to infuse this tale with all of the gritty, harsh reality that women in abusive relationships deal with every day. This book is not for the faint of heart, so recognize that you are officially warned: it contains violent content.

Domestic violence destroys lives, and when the opportunity presented itself for me to possibly do something that could help prevent it, I jumped at the chance. I wrote this story in hopes of showing the world just how wrong it is.

If you or someone you know is being abused, call The National Domestic Violence Hotline immediately at 1-800-799-SAFE (7233).

10/17/2012

ALL WORDS WRITTEN AS DICTATED BY ME ARE ENTIRELY FACTUAL AS I SAW EVENTS TRANSPIRE. 'FOREVER SCARRED' — THE JOHN WAYNE BOBBITT STORY — IS AS TRUE AS POSSIBLE AND I FULLY STAND BEHIND THIS ACCOUNT, AS I WILL ATTEST TO IN ANY & ALL INTERVIEWS.

(Signed statement from John Wayne Bobbitt)

Chapter 1

With one malicious flick of her knife wielding wrist, I was callously thrust into the worldwide spotlight. The sound resonated through the warm night air eerily similar to the snapping of a large rubber band. Instantly, I sprang from my slumber in excruciating pain. Rolling off the bed, I doubled over onto the floor. Frantically I clutched at my groin! Warm blood was all that filled my hands, and immediately I realized there was something missing. She did it! She really did it! It was gone! The night was June 23, 1993, and in only a few short days, my name was more widely known around the world than the President of the United States.

I was born on the outskirts of Niagara Falls, New York, to a loving mother and a degenerate alcoholic father. We were poor, and our surroundings were deplorable. We lived in the ghetto among the black population of our area, and hence, we were always treated like outsiders. My first memory would forever shape my future mindset toward others.

It was a crisp autumn afternoon when my mother staggered into our yard bloody and abused. She collapsed at the feet of my father causing me to look up from my toys. Moaning in anguish, my father quickly dropped to his knees in an effort to see what had happened to her. Everything went into slow motion. My innocence was shattered once my eardrums heard the words come out of her mouth.

"THEY JUST RAPED ME!"

She screamed so loudly that it sent a terrible feeling shivering down my spine. All of the hairs on the back of my neck stood as a prickling sensation ran over my flesh. I did not know why, but I began to cry. Terror seized my fragile mind as darkness crept its way across me. Our yard immediately transformed from my bright, vibrant playground into a barren wasteland. I felt pure evil encompass me as vicious claws scratched at my flesh. I was paralyzed in fear as my bladder released a torrent of urine. There I stood, cold and alone, only a few feet away from my parents. I was enduring a violent and tumultuous demonic onslaught and it seemed no one would help me. My mind splintered as everything buckled into the void. I retreated into my subconscious. This would forever scar my simple mind. I experienced a horrific assault of epic proportion. No matter how much I have tried over the years, I have never been able to forget it. I was only three years old, but I remember it as if it was yesterday.

My father clutched my mother. Her words became indistinguishable as she lamented. Tears streamed like the mighty Niagara River only a few miles away as she released her pain on my immature ears. My heart broke as the person I loved most in the world lay helpless and abused. I could do nothing.

The warmth from the sunshine dissipated, as the cold winds of man's inhumanity to man blew across my flesh. I was swallowed in the abyss. Marauding souls that lurked in the shadows stole from my mother what she was unwilling to give. Depraved villains populated our surroundings and we had no escape. We were forced by poverty to coexist with society's dregs and we compromised comforts to live. At three years old, this is what I came to realize.

It seemed as if the pale sunlight no longer glistened as it once did across my mother's hair. Now the muffled sound of suffering escaped from her lips. My father held her tightly in his arms. Frozen speechless, I stood silent in front of them. Never before had my infantile brain been bombarded with such ferocity, the world's cruelty invaded my mind. Only half did I comprehend the travesty that had befallen my mother, but this experience would tarnish any and all of my relationships from this day forth.

I stood perplexed at what to do. Did I approach my parents or stand back from the pain unfolding in front of me? Every second that passed lasted an eternity, and the foul stench of misery filled the air. I was utterly lost in the wake of my parent's sea of disgrace. I drifted along aimlessly as the choppy waters of uncertainty carried me further from the shore. Standing in my front yard, I felt a million miles from home, yet I was only a few feet from the front door.

A demoralizing slap from my father resurrected my mother from her hysteria. The high pitch frequency of her disgrace was heard down the block. Darkened shadows of neighborhood pedestrians loomed ominously as they gawked and stared. They were simply casualty vampires, people who were entertained by the misery of others.

Not a single person approached to help. They pretended not to notice. I received my first glimpse of just how cruel the world could be. While my mother frantically wailed, people passed in front of our home as if it were just an ordinary day. The pathetic display played out for all to see, yet no one acknowledged a thing. My self-imposed isolation imprisoned me with grief.

Tears welled up in my eyes and caused my vision to blur. Sunlight reflected off of the saline running down my cheeks. I desperately tried to make sense of all of this in my head. Noticing some flowering weeds that had sprouted along the neighbor's house, I stumbled across the lawn toward them. I reached down with my hand and pulled them from the ground. Sharp thistles lined the entire length of the stem, cutting into my young, delicate flesh. With a sudden release from the earth's clutches, I held the dirt clumped prickly weeds in my hand. Tiny droplets of blood could be seen on my palms through the foliage.

In a pathetic attempt to remedy my mother's misery, I walked across the lawn to her. As my father held her in his arms, I extended my bouquet toward her and gently tapped her on the arm. In her delirium she briefly paused for air. Looking toward me, she struggled to see through her tears. Wrestling with the glare from the sun she looked deep into my eyes. Focusing on the flowers in my hand, she accepted them, and continued to sob as she kissed my bloody hand, "You are my sunshine," she gasped.

From that day forth she called me, "Sunshine." For years she tried to wash my mind of the filth of that day but I have always remembered it. My mother's life was always filled with pain. I have never been able to forget those events.

Forgiveness is a beautiful concept because it washes away hurt and animosity from one's heart. Forgetting, on the other hand, is an almost impossible task. My life was forever altered on that day. Thinking back now, I can see that bouquet of flowering weeds in my tiny blood soaked hand as clearly as the day that I held them. Something inside me would forever ache for peace. My mother was never the same again after they stole her virtue, and my father never looked favorably upon her again. From that day forward, his abuse toward us made our lives a living hell.

The sun disappeared over our house for the next few years. After the rape of my mother, my father's cold hard, violent demeanor intensified during the rest of the time that he was with us. Alcohol fueled his anger and became the prime motivator as he wreaked havoc in our home. A pathetic, wretched man, he staggered around furiously, waiting to discipline with an iron fist. He would punch you just to prompt you to change the television channel for him. His evil reign was unrelenting, with Satan riding shotgun. Misery was all that surrounded me. I tried to tread lightly every day through the hell where I slept. I lived in constant fear of the fierce retribution that would befall me if I upset him. My memory is hazy from all of the torment I endured, as I am sure you can understand. I was the mere shell of a child. My mother was incapable of coping with the emotions lain at her feet. Her immature mind was full of shame over the indignity that had befallen her, and her heart was weak. My father blamed her for all of the events that day. It did not take long until finally, he would leave forever.

My mother only had a sixth grade education, so she was fundamentally a child herself, now trying to raise three children on her own. There were my two younger brothers, my mother, and I, totally alone. It is times like these that test the mettle of a person. This early portion of a life is when a child develops their core value system. Perhaps this is the rudimentary cause for my gross lack of moral fiber. My mother failed miserably when it came to instilling values.

In those early years, I found comfort in my brothers. Where my mother failed in teaching us coping skills, I sought solace in the companionship of my siblings. Though we were young, we looked out for one another and though we were hungry, we were hungry together. They say, "Misery loves company." Joseph and Ernest were the company for my misery. We would be lucky to eat daily only if an aunt or uncle came by and dropped off some food. We were dirty, and we were hungry, but through all of this, we were together.

When you grow up knowing nothing but hunger, it is a lowly existence. However, when you do not have contentment to gauge your hunger against, you just do not know any better. It has to do with sheer ignorance. The fact that I just was not aware of my reality was a blessing in disguise.

Suffering and loss are key components necessary for one to learn the plight of the human condition. Without true sorrow how would one understand pure joy? Without struggle how would one comprehend conquest? These are the thoughts I use every day to understand and forgive my parents for what I endured as a child. A child's mind, much like their body, is extremely resilient. I was denied most of the necessities one needs to exist, but I made it out alive. For that, I am thankful. Time without something, and this applies to almost anything, is the best way to learn how good that something really is. I was a product of my environment, and my environment was poverty.

My mother's lack of intelligence made her incapable of finding work. She begged, bartered, and even sometimes, stole. Once she was caught stealing in McLeod's Grocery over on Ontario Avenue and 11th Street. Mrs. McLeod told her that she could take what she needed on credit, and for a short time after, that is how we lived. We ate macaroni and cheese, hotdogs, and occasionally some white bread, and always on credit. Truthfully, looking back, our bill was never paid in full. The kindness of good people is a beautiful thing, and Mrs. McLeod was exactly that, a beautiful thing. Thanks to her we were able to eat on a somewhat regular basis. Without her, I would have never lived long enough to become the brunt of a million jokes, and unlike Lorena, Mrs. McLeod never cut me off.

Chapter 2

It takes fortitude to overcome the obstacles in life. First and foremost is the perception of others. If you are true to yourself, then you do not need to concern yourself with what others think of you. This is why you know very few, if any, truly happy people. My dilemma is that I do care what people think about me, and I want to clear my name. That is why I am telling all in this book: what I did and why I did it.

"The truth shall set you free."

I want to clear my conscience, to be finally free and clear of my guilt. I want to help people see that honesty, and admitting your faults, is the way to forgiveness. I need to share my story with the world no matter how awful it makes me look. It was difficult over the years to just stand by and let the parasites spread rumor and conjecture. But this is something I brought upon myself. I blame no one. I was told what to say in court because of the headlines that go along with a successful defense on a worldwide stage. This is what has haunted me ever since.

I was acquitted of 'Marital Sexual Abuse' at my trial in 1993, and truth be told, I am guilty. I did force Lorena, on multiple occasions, to have sex against her will. There, I said it. Now here we are twenty years later and I am finally able to admit this publicly. My heart has suffered as much over the years as my penis suffered on the night of June 23, 1993. I now ask for forgiveness from Lorena and the world.

Most people in society blindly follow the masses in a vain attempt to keep the status quo. If someone they perceive to be important states their opinion publicly, the sheep of the world line up to follow. It is few and far between when you see innovators blaze trails in uncharted territories. No one ever steps forth and takes accountability for their evil actions. Who, if anyone says, "I did this terrible thing and I ask for the world to forgive me." If anyone has, I didn't hear about it.

How do I right this wrong that I did? The first step is my full admission of guilt that will grace these pages. I will tell it all, as it happened. I was a young and foolish twenty-something year old Marine. I married a woman so that she could obtain her citizenship. This was a decision I would pay for, for the rest of my life. I did not think about consequences or repercussions. I thought about sex and the promise she made me: if I married her, she would give me all of the sex I wanted, whenever I wanted it. That was the deal. To a twenty year old this sounded like the perfect arrangement.

You know what they say about Marine Corps grunts, "Young, dumb, and full of cum."

I was the epitome of that phrase, with a major emphasis on the dumb part! Prepare to step into the mind of an asshole. Because that's what you're going to do when you read this book. At least I am honest enough to forewarn you. This book is not going to be a bunch of jumbled up stories proclaiming my innocence, in fact, quite the contrary. It will be a full admission of my guilt and the craziness that followed my subsequent meteoric rise to fame. You will see firsthand what happens when a simple man is forced under the microscope of worldwide media scrutiny.

In 1993, I was a douchebag. Finally, after all of these years, I can take accountability for that. For the past twenty years I have allowed the stench of shame to fill the air around me. Do I truly deserve to be forgiven? With all of the hurt I have done, can I forgive myself? My soul has been tormented for as far back as I can remember, and I just want a break away from all of the pain. I guess I will have to wait and see what you, the reader thinks.

I grew up hard on those cold nights in Western New York, without a father to guide me. To be brutally honest, I have done many bad things in my life, but since I have never killed anyone, I feel that I have paid the ultimate price for my sin. What I have received as punishment has often made death sound better. I was emasculated on a worldwide stage.

What I will openly admit to now, is something that I had so vehemently denied before. I had sex with Lorena against her will when we were married, on multiple occasions, and for that, she chopped off my dick. What else can I say about the situation? I was wrong. When I was in The Marine Corps, I was nuts. The government had brainwashed me to be a fighting machine, and I was too dumb to compartmentalize my emotions. I was warped from the pressures of the military and the scars of my childhood. With everything weighing so heavily on my feeble mind, I crumbled.

I was a Marine Corp grunt with a sack full of testosterone and a mind full of Uncle Sam. I made foolish mistakes because my naive mind was too stupid to see the error in my ways. Lorena was forced to deal with a troubled young man, and for all of the wrongs I did to her, I am truly sorry. No one deserves the pain I caused, especially not Lorena.

And as for my punishment, I am the brunt of a million dick jokes.

Chapter 3

Alone with no fatherly protector to watch over me, the real nightmare began. Looking out into the frightening world ahead of me, I was overwhelmed with a feeling of helplessness. When you are a child, the simplicity of your mindset can make even the smallest problem feel like the largest conundrum. That is how my life seemed after my father left, like nothing was ever going to be okay again. Not that my life before was all that pleasurable when he was around, but now, I just knew things were really going to suck.

I silently pleaded for help over the next year, but it never arrived. Then magically, as if God himself decided to answer my prayers, my uncle asked my mother if he could raise us. He obviously thought he could do a much better job. My mother was incapable of handling her responsibilities as a parent and gladly accepted my uncle's offer. We did not see much of her after we moved in with them. The bitter charm of solitude would be the death of my mother. It ended up driving her into an early grave in the form of a heart attack. I would love to sing praise in my mother's defense, but that would be a very short song.

Life had dealt her a poor hand of cards, and she folded. On the other hand, I was in for the long haul.

My uncle did not have riches, but he did have something almost as valuable… food. The night we moved in was the first time in my life I had ever seen lettuce. Salad was a bit of a shock in the beginning since I thought it was weeds from the lawn. Thanks to my aunt and uncle, I soon became used to all of the food groups being represented at the dinner table. I also acquired three new brothers in the move, Bill, Tim, and Jeff. They were my cousins by blood, but became brothers in my heart.

Sometimes I wonder what my life would have been like if I had begun with a stable home environment. Would I have still ended up making national headlines? Being the casualty of one of the most shocking crimes in American history is a difficult burden. My mundane life suddenly transformed from obscurity to intense media scrutiny, overnight. Every news station across the globe covered the story. It was a runaway train and I was along for the ride.

The fervency in which the news outlets carried my tale of woe across the airwaves was so intense, it was rocket fueled! The day after Lorena maimed me, my two brothers Bill and Tim sped across the country from Upstate New York, to be by my side at the hospital in Virginia. It was then that they were pulled over by an Ohio State Trooper.

The trooper said, "What the hell is so damn important that you boys have to be driving 100 mph through my state?"

They responded, "John Wayne Bobbitt is our brother and we are driving to see him in the hospital."

"You boys tell him we are all praying for him. I will give you an escort to the state line!"

Then he ran back to his squad car, hit the wailers, and led them on their way. That is how quickly the story swept across the country. Twelve hours after Lorena cut off my penis, my brothers were being escorted across the state of Ohio by the police. The story exploded all around me like a cannon shot, and I was caught in its crosshairs. My brain was bombarded from every angle. The shock of it all was just as massive as the trauma that my body had sustained. I was a sheep among wolves as news outlets clamored for the exclusive.

I must say, the mockery I received in the media was debilitating. My inability to properly articulate a response made me a laughing stock publicly. I was berated on every news station worldwide. This was done simply for ratings. News outlets want sensationalized stories that sweep the nation. My story had newspapers and magazines flying off the racks.

This entire event proved just how morally bankrupt our society is. To find humor in the mutilation of one's genitalia, most importantly my genitalia, is just perverse. I could fill an entire book with a list of what was wrong with taking pleasure in seeing my suffering, but that would be pointless. Every time I hear someone laugh at me, I feel myself die a little inside, but it is the only way I know how to cope with the situation.

"If you can't beat 'em, you may as well join 'em."

There is a laundry list of John Wayne Bobbitt jokes I have been forced to hear. And it's just not that funny when you're the punch line!

In the fallout of the tragic night of June 23, 1993,

Lorena was also catapulted into the worldwide spotlight. Lorena's feminist martyrdom has dubbed her a pop culture icon, where simply the mention of the name John Wayne Bobbitt, invokes a somewhat comedic response. Sincerely though, I am glad for her success, and I wish her all of the best in the future.

I have come to learn many things in my time here on earth, and most importantly, now I understand that honesty is the best policy. In order to find true peace and serenity you must first be honest with yourself. If you want to achieve a higher sense of consciousness, you must admit all of your wrong doings. Once you do you are free of regret, only then will true happiness be found. Offer apologies to those you have wronged, and then it is up to them to forgive you. The ball is in their court. It takes far more energy to harbor ill will than it does to forgive. I have forgiven everyone who has wronged me in my life, and as I will tell in this book, there are many. But we will cover that later.

To truly appreciate my thinking you need to understand how I was raised. The next several years were spent living with my aunt and uncle. As I grew, I learned that a real man sticks around and raises his children, or in this case, other people's children. There are very few people you will meet in life that you can truly count on. My aunt and uncle were two such luxuries. We were subsisting on minimal finances with so many people living in the house. My uncle stepped up and did what he had to do to fund our blended family.

My uncle had several "boosters" who would bring stolen merchandise to him that he would then buy. This is called fencing. Let me break down this bit of criminality: you buy a stolen item from a thief for one price, and then you sell it to another person for a higher price. My uncle was a fence, a man who deals in the resale of stolen property. Being surrounded by a constant criminal element growing up did something to alter my views on how one might choose to pay the bills. My uncle had many mouths to feed, and as you know several were not his, so I do not fault him for having to cut corners from time to time. This may be part of the reason I am a bit jaded toward crime. I too have had a brush with the law on a few occasions. I see that larceny is in my blood. There are many poor decisions that I have made in my life that have resulted in multiple arrests.

I understand that the purchase and sale of stolen goods is wrong, but when I was young, it was just commonplace. The food I ate was always directly or indirectly funded by theft. For a brief period of time, my uncle tried to feed us with good intentions, but we were all still hungry afterwards. It was that crime filled our dinner table and I enjoyed eating. Coming from a house with no food, to a house with food, was a blessing, and however it arrived was fine with me. If you have never experienced true hunger, you will never understand. It is only when you can weigh the morality of theft, versus the longing for food, that you can grasp the concept.

"Desperate times call for desperate measures."

Living at my aunt and uncle's house, I developed a moral ambivalence toward the crime that funded our family's betterment. Sure I knew what my uncle did was immoral, but it fed us. My brain continually warred with my stomach over right and wrong, theft or food, but my appetite was always the trump card. My stomach won that argument every time.

So that is how it went over the next several years of

my life. Boosters showed up at our house at all hours of the day and night. My uncle purchased their stolen products for later resale time and time again. I saw it as often as the sun rose over our tiny one bathroom tenement. We all resided together, and our bond was even closer than our tightly packed accommodations.

Our house was a layover for wayward relatives during my youth. It was commonplace to find one or more aunts, uncles, or cousins, staying rent free for months at a time. My uncle was a sucker for a sob story, and when someone needed a place to flop, they knew where to come. It was a relative such as this, who was the perpetrator of the most sinister crimes against me. Between my brothers and me, no one knows for sure who he chose as his first victim, but since I was the eldest, at the ripe age of five, we think it must have been me.

It was an eerily quiet night when he first crept in through the darkness of my room. I was awakened by the feel of cold wrinkly flesh as his hand slipped under the sheets and the scent of alcohol oozed off his breath. I furrowed my brow in confusion as his hand invaded the pelvic region of my tiny pajama bottoms. I remember it as if it was yesterday, the hollow feeling in the pit of my stomach that began to echo through my brain. All of my whimpers were cried out in vain; they were never answered. His excessive indulgences were catered to at our house with so many young boys. While my aunt and uncle were at work or at night while they slept, he binged, feasting on our flesh as often as he wished.

Every chance this sick, sexual sadist could get his greasy hands on me, he did. While I was supposed to be developing my senses of smell, touch, and taste, I was busy instead learning shame. Believe me, shame was working overtime! Even at my young age I knew how wrong this was, but what could I do? Every time it happened I would cry myself to sleep.

In the beginning, this degenerate fuck would isolate me from my siblings and abuse me at will. He would satisfy all of his sadistic fetishes using my body as his personal playground. Sometimes he would piss all over me and then spend the next hour licking my body clean, always focusing the extent of his energy on my penis. Other times he would beat me while he held me down and sodomized me. He was a sick and depraved individual who was aroused by hurting me. The first time he had his way with me, he tore my anus so badly I limped around the house unable to sit for a week. When he penetrated me, it felt like shards of glass being forced inside. I literally heard the tearing reverberate through my body. He liked to punch me in the kidneys as he savagely pounded away on my tiny backside. He called it, "Time for boom-boom on your back side." He was the worst sort of person. He laughed while I cried. On bad days, I can still hear him calling out to me. Sometimes I wake in cold sweats. I do not think I will ever get over what he did to me.

When someone molests a child there is usually the illusion of seduction, whether it is done by offering them some much needed attention, buying his affection, or grandiose promises of happiness. This was not the case in my house. There was no sweet talk and sugar kisses; this was rape. Rape in the first degree! He was always careful never to rip my pajamas, but I still remember the tearing sound resonating through my body the first time he penetrated me. My virgin cavity was left hollowed out and blood soaked, leaking his toxic seed. Every time he paid me a visit I limped for days afterward. However, the resilience of my infantile flesh was to his benefit. As we only bathed once a week, his damage went largely unnoticed for what seemed like an eternity.

His visits became more frequent and more brazen with each passing day. After a while he began to make us watch him sodomize each other. I suppose in an effort to increase his pleasure he would terrorize us simultaneously. The low guttural moans and the sounds of pained anguish filled the air as tears streamed down our tiny faces. It was even worse seeing my brothers endure the torture than it was to experience it. As he pounded us savagely, the others were forced to watch feeling utterly helpless. It was monumentally horrific, and I have never been able to forget the events I endured. His depraved fixation on pedophilia awards him the luxury of being, the sickest man I have ever known.

Then one day, he went to the pastor of our church with a full admission of his crimes. He was removed from our home without incident as part of the despicable deal agreed upon between the pastor and my uncle. There were no legal charges ever pressed, and though we never saw him again, we were left with a lifetime of pain.

Life seemed to improve as I went through middle

school and then into senior high. I was on the wrestling and swim teams. I excelled at both, but it never took me anywhere. Back then they did not have Attention Deficit/ Hyperactivity Disorder... we were just stupid. After sneaking past graduation with piss-poor grades, I needed to find a way to support myself. I was eighteen years old and oblivious to the world. So I kicked around for a year until I decided to join the U.S. Marine Corps. It would only be a few more years until I would be known the world over, as the ultimate asshole.

Chapter 4

Shortly after enlisting with the Marines, I found my naïve ass standing smack dab in the middle of the Parris Island, South Carolina, reception center. Only moments after disembarking from the plane, a roughneck in a stern voice bellowed, "Listen up... you needle dick faggots better fall in line! My name is Sergeant Williams, but you will all answer me Sir, yes Sir. Now sound off like you got a pair when you're spoken too! Do you understand me recruits? You will follow my orders like they came down from on high, directly from the good Lord himself. Now am I perfectly clear to you fucking maggots?"

"Sir yes Sir!" I shouted at the top of my lungs.

It became crystal clear to me in a matter of moments that this was going to be a long ten weeks. It was just like you have seen in every war movie that showed basic training. It was hard. Every step I took over the next several weeks someone around me was yelling at me about something. That is the way they condition a new soldier's mind to be able to deal with the constant bombardment of battle. Just like famed behaviorist Pavlov's theory of conditioned response worked for dogs, they believe that through repetition a soldier will learn the proper behavior. They were right too. It was not long until I was a well-oiled, order following, killing machine. When they said jump, I said, "How high?"

My next two and a half months were spent running here, running there, running with things strapped to my back, and running with things in my arms. Like an '80's pop star, I was doing the running man all over the base. Occasionally I thought about home, but rarely since I was so physically worn out and mentally exhausted at all times. At this point in my life, this was the most challenging thing I had ever experienced. And after what seemed like an eternity, it was graduation day.

Having already been through the ringer in my day, I was truly proud for the first time in my life. Looking like a Duke in my dress blues, I felt like a real man. Finally all of my hard work had paid off, and I was now a part of something.

'Semper Fidelis,' is Latin for, "Always Faithful."

That is the motto of The United States Marine

Corps, and now this was my motto. I was now officially, of the few, the proud, The Marines.

I was assigned to the 3531 Motor Transport Division. I was happy to be finally free and clear of that know-nothing town, Niagara Falls. I moved to Manassas, Virginia. I was going to do everything that I could to be a celebrated soldier, so that my family would be proud of me. I suppose it stemmed back to when I was abused, for there was a deep longing in my heart to make them see me as a man. I truthfully do not think I will ever get over being sodomized. I have tried to forget what happened to me, but I just cannot.

Scandal is fodder for the miscreants populating the globe. People love to see others suffer, so much so in fact, that reports claimed sixty percent of the American population ravenously followed my story and the trial. Everyone enjoyed watching my misery, and bloodsuckers lurked around every corner. Never have I heard more disturbing words spoken of anyone in history, than those the media so callously spewed about me. It was brutality at its rawest and most primal form. It was equal to clubbing a seal viciousness, and I was just as defenseless. The world sought to project all of its anger upon me, and I was forced to endure it. Nothing under the sun could have ever prepared me for what I faced.

You see, growing up I did not receive the proper tools to learn to cope with trauma. I did not have the luxury of a stable home environment in my early years. Because of this my development suffered severely. Truthfully, I don't think any man on the planet, no matter how he was raised, has the tools to cope with having their penis cut off in the middle of the night and then tossed into a vacant field. In addition, due to my lack of finesse, I had a hard time expressing myself to the media. Now add to this Post-Traumatic Stress Disorder from being emasculated, and you have a recipe for disaster.

Post-Traumatic Stress Disorder and its symptoms can debilitate a person beyond repair. Constant nightmares of the incident, coupled with my memories of the sexual abuse I experienced as a child plagued me, causing sleep deprivation. This all culminated in delusional thoughts and paranoia. Any and all of my responses to the media seemed contrived. No one ever empathized or tried to sympathize with my situation. Everyone just made a joke out of it. In my fragile state, I made stupid statements that only furthered public opinion that I was retarded. Realize also that anyone who aligned themselves with me did it strictly for monetary gain. It was a media circus and I was inconsequentially discarded once the novelty wore off, but, my problems still remained.

When you face the intense media scrutiny that I was forced to endure, coupled with the trauma of having my penis severed, you cannot help but become somewhat stunted mentally. The residual Post Traumatic Stress Disorder I suffered was horrendous. I don't know which was worse, the sleepless nights, or when I did manage to get any sleep, the horrible realistic, ultra-graphic nightmares that I had were like living the event over again. Every time my eyes closed I was petrified that I would go through it all again.

My life was in a constant state of turmoil. Regardless of whether I was home alone or out in public, I was suffering. I knew deep down in my heart that I would have to take accountability someday for my wrongs against Lorena. Now I just hope she can forgive me. I was so young and foolish back then. If I could go back in time, I would change everything. I just hope that she knows how sorry I am. I truly loved her.

    After being assigned to the motor transport division, my next six months of time in the Marines flew by like shit through a goose. The devotion toward my military career showed in everything I did. Whether we were on a rifle range or a long run, I gave it my all, and that made the Sergeants like me. Whatever I was told to do, I did it well. I was a physical specimen unrivaled by any other man in my squad. I could do push-ups as easily as others chewed gum, and when it came to running, I was like the wind. I excelled in every aspect of training. I paid close attention to the instructors and quickly was singled out for use in demonstrations. I carefully studied the moves that were being executed against me, and I quickly mastered all of them under such clever tutelage. I was slowly but surely being transformed into a killing machine, one lesson at a time. They showed you how to incapacitate a foe, then to kill. And during all of this training, there was an underlying theme that largely went unnoticed: they were brain washing you not to feel any sympathy or remorse for your enemy. They were creating a literal monster that they could sic on whomever they chose. You were slowly but surely becoming an expendable assassin that they could send to do their bidding. Throughout all of my training, they had surreptitiously made me a brainwashed, emotionless soldier, who was capable of unspeakable acts at any given time. This is what they wanted, and this is what I became. (This is why they use eighteen and nineteen year old boys as soldiers, because grown men would never fall for the bullshit brainwashing that they do.) With all of the vast resources at the military's disposal, they spared no expense. Soldiers have to be stone cold killers. There is no need or want for sensitivity on the battlefield. The military needs monsters that are capable of committing atrocities. With my somewhat diminished intelligence, maybe I became a little more of this monster than they set out to create.

Chapter 5

About six months into my tour, I was invited to attend the Marine Corps Ball in Quantico, Virginia. Thinking back in hindsight, I should have burned that invitation! But as we all know, hindsight is 20/20; present sight, on the other hand, has been known to be a bit sketchy from time to time. Booze, dress blues, and dancing… I assumed attending the gala was my duty. When I first arrived with a few of my buddies, I was actually a bit bored. Then it happened. My life changed forever when I caught my first glimpse of her. Love walked into the room for me. Never before or since has one woman so effortlessly captivated me. Instantly I was awestruck, hanging on bated breath. My mouth went dry and my knees weakened. My stomach rumbled with nervous anticipation, but I could not stop my feet from walking toward her.

Through absolutely no effort of my own, I ended up standing smack dab in front of her. I fumbled a bit while I sweated profusely. I dug down deep inside of my heart until I found the strength to ask her to dance. Surprisingly, it was like trying to get an audience with a queen: this person had to confer with that chaperone, and he had to ask another guy, until finally she was permitted to put her tiny hand in mine. For one brief and fleeting moment, the shame and disgrace that have followed me around my entire life vanished. I felt complete and utter peace for the first time I can remember.

My heart's palpitations would have fooled you into thinking I was on a ten mile run. After some clever navigating through the crowded ballroom we arrived at the dance floor. Slowly, I turned to face her. The way the light cascaded on her shoulders, glistening off of her olive complexion, was something to behold. Her long dark hair flowed effortlessly down to the nape of her neck, and the scent she omitted was sweet. The darkness of her eyes added a certain mystery and an engaging allure to this newfound apple of my eye. My attraction to her was instantaneous, but the punishment I would receive for wronging her would be severe, and last a lifetime.

As she turned toward me to begin our first waltz, we clung to one another with nervous tension. She trembled in my arms as we began awkwardly to traverse the dance floor. She hovered alongside my muscular frame and seemed to complete a missing piece of me. I felt like a god amongst men as we lost ourselves in the magic of the moment. Never before had I felt such an intuitive connection to someone. We were two long lost souls who were finally united, and it was pure bliss.

Not a word was spoken between us as we both felt what was not said. She was elegance in its purest form, and I became intoxicated by her musk. The delicate fragrance of blossoming love was in the air, and my nostrils gasped hungrily. I felt beauty exuding from her as we lost ourselves in one another. I was in heaven. My mind was swirling and our bodies were twirling as we danced away the night. When the first song stopped we continued dancing for a few seconds before we even realized the music was no longer playing. By the time the band took its first break I was totally and completely in love with her. I had only one small problem… we had yet to speak a word.

As the band dispersed, I decided to try and woo her with some clever conversation. My persuasion quickly fell short as soon as it began.

"Wow, you sure can dance. I hope I wasn't too clumsy for you. Would you like to get some refreshments?"

Then it happened. In broken dialect she spoke, "No speak English too good."

Immediately a confused and embarrassed look appeared on her face. She began to fidget and her discomfort was apparent. "I go," she spouted as she began to make a dash toward her chaperones across the ballroom. I recognized her discomfort and quickly tried to console her.

I grabbed her arm as she attempted to flee and persuaded her to stay, "It's ok that you don't speak good English, because neither do I. Let's dance some more and forget about talking for now."

She nodded in agreement and we did just that. Once the band began to play again, we continued our magical dance all through the night. It was just her and I. The people around us all disappeared into the mist. We forgot about our language barrier and just listened to the music of our hearts serenading our minds. There were no countries of origin or foreign languages to speak, there was only our attraction for one another. It was the kind of romance that only comes once in a lifetime... if you are lucky that is.

I remember it was like floating, high above the clouds, not thinking about anything at all. I was completely satisfied and I did not want it to end. I walked her back to her chaperones and politely asked if I could see her again. They obliged me with a phone number and a warning, "You would have to meet her family, and it would be up to them to approve courting their daughter."

That night after leaving The Marine Corps Ball, I knew I had met the woman of my dreams. I think I had an erection the entire time we were dancing. I could not wait to see her again. My heart was racing just from imagining what being intimate with her would be like. The whole way home I kept sniffing my lapels because they smelled like her. After getting back to my barracks, I stripped down naked and masturbated while smelling my jacket. I imagined her beautiful body naked before me with her delicious olive skin glistening with sweat as I made sweet love to her. The rhythm of our hearts driving the tempo as I penetrated her, switching to new positions as we writhed and contorted in a sexual frenzy. Finally, in my mind, after a series of deep, savage thrusts, we both experienced debilitating orgasms.

What is most ironic about that now is that when Lorena was arrested for my mutilation, the first thing she told investigators was, "He always have orgasm. He never waits for me to orgasm. He is a greedy lover."

In actuality, only one of us ever had orgasms and that same one was left severed! But that is all going to come later, as for right now, our relationship was perfect.

You see, many people have a problem with honesty. While it may seem complex at first, it is a simple philosophy. You must be forthright, able to forgo your deceitful ways, and become somewhat of an open book. It is only when you no longer have anything left to hide, that you can truly begin to live your life. I have come to the realization that the only way for me to be forgiven for all that I have done is to admit all of my wrongs, regardless of how they make me look. Only out of the clash of destructive forces does the opportunity to create special present itself. This is something I have learned in life, and it is something that gives me hope for the redemption that I so desperately seek.

Chapter 6

On August 25, 1814, a woman named Ann Crampton, 40 years old, was hanged at Dryburn Prison, Durham, England, for cutting off her philandering husband's penis while he slept. She was subsequently convicted of 'cutting and maiming,' and executed for her crime.

Isn't it remarkable what a couple hundred years can do for the public perception of a crime? Where Mrs. Crampton was inconsequentially dispatched for mutilating her husband's genitalia, Lorena has been celebrated the world over as a feminist martyr in the media. I find it deplorable that such a double standard exists in our society. If a man was to do something even remotely similar, i.e. female castration, he would no doubt receive a hefty prison sentence. Regardless of the legal ramifications, I am sure the victim would not have hundreds of protesters congregating outside of the courthouse, shouting angry slogans as the victim ascended the steps each day for trial as I did. It seems ironic to think that we are actually advancing in our society and becoming more civilized.

Quite the contrary, in many cases, we have resorted to barbarism.

The celebration of Lorena's act was simply ludicrous, but the media gobbled it up like a turkey dinner on Thanksgiving. The feminist displays around the courthouse during my trial were simply disgusting. Angry demonstrators waved severed dildos adorned with fake blood as I was led into trial. It was a media circus, and I was the villainous clown. Female activists mocked my pain and slanderous insults were hurled in my direction as, still healing, I struggled to walk up the courthouse steps in the interest of jurisprudence.

What all of these protesters did not understand, was that I never wanted Lorena in prison. I loved her. I wanted to crawl under a rock and escape the continual media scrutiny that plagued my meager existence. But it only got worse. Death threats and hate mail arrived daily. I was cracking at the seams, and there was no one to help me. My mind was tattered and confused. I silently pleaded for help, but it never came. I was alone in my own war zone, caught in the crossfire. I'm not sure that my mind can ever recover from what I experienced. I spent my days wishing to be anywhere else. I just wanted to step away from the madness and have peace for five fucking minutes. By circumstance, I was forced to endure it, but I should probably get back to my story.

For the next six months after the Marine Corp Ball, Lorena and I dated, but we were always chaperoned. She began attending the community college to study English, but even with her growing knowledge of the language, it was an unusual courtship, as you can imagine. Always being accompanied by strangers made our relationship feel forced, and it was difficult. At the time though, this woman was everything to me.

We were always kept at a distance, and our flirtations were in secret. On every possible occasion however, we enjoyed playful banter and a plethora of sexual innuendo. Lorena had informed me that she was a virgin, and I was bewitched, to say the least. As things progressed in our relationship, she began working at a hair salon for a woman named Janet. She liked the work and Janet quickly became her closest friend. Her family's trust in Janet was the escape we so desperately needed from their watchful eyes.

Soon thereafter, Janet began to take us places, and we were free to pursue our lustful wants for one another. It was not long after we began being intimate. I have to say it was certainly worth the wait! If you are unwilling to take a risk, you will never receive a reward. One thing about our relationship was that we had passion from the start. I know that that life is far too short to live without it. A passionless relationship is like a meal with no taste, a day with no sun, or a lie with no truth. If you do not have your true love, you simply have filler. You need to set forth from your humdrum complacency, and find the Yin to your Yang. It is worth risking everything. If you settle in life you never get to realize your full capacity to love. It is like only putting half of the recommended air into a tire on your car, it's always a bit flat. Life is about actions and reactions. If you do not give out, you don't get back.

I remember the first time Lorena and I were intimate, as if it was yesterday. It was just past our sixth month mark of being together, and we were both spending the night at Janet's apartment. Of course Lorena's parents were unaware that I was there; otherwise we would never have been able to pull it off. Janet was sleeping as Lorena happened to be doing the dishes from dinner earlier that evening. Janet had a free housemaid in Lorena, and let me tell you, she took full advantage. Janet had her cleaning the salon during the day and then her own house at night.

I noticed her by the sink scrubbing dishes when I walked into the kitchen. Her little bottom was wiggling with each forceful stroke as she attempted to scour the burnt residue from whatever subpar meal Janet had cauterized to the pan. I dimmed the lights with the round knob that was next to the entryway into the kitchen. I glided up behind her as she continued the daunting task of trying to salvage the pan from a final resting place at the local landfill. I placed my hands on her slender hips and pushed my pelvis firmly against her buttocks. Removing my left hand from its clutch, I brought it across her back and delicately moved her hair from her shoulder, exposing the nape of her neck. Her smooth, olive skin glistened in the soft light as the sound of running water soothed our senses. I began gently to lick and suck at the base of her neck while reaching both of my hands around from behind toward the crotch of her skirt. Once my hands reached their destination, she let out a whimper as I continued playfully taunting the back of her neck.

Overwhelmed with pleasure, she paused from her labor and reached back with her right hand. Clutching the back of my head by a handful of hair, she pulled my head closer. With smooth gyrations from her hips accompanying my hands vigorously working on her groin, she began to breathe deeper and more savagely. Continuing my onslaught from the front with my hands, and the rear with my pelvis, I humped her in rhythmic time. My full-on invasion was eminent.

Her vagina had begun to leak moisture through her panties and I could feel the heat through the fabric of her skirt. She let out a sound that was somewhere between a sigh and a growl as she quickly turned to face me. She grabbed the back of my head with both hands and dug her fingernails deep into my skull. She jumped up and wrapped her legs around my waist in one fluid motion. I effortlessly set her atop the counter as she kissed me intensely. The sounds of heavy breathing and lips smacking filled the air. The smell of sex was palpable as the steam from the running water carried the scent to our nostrils.

I reached down with one free hand and unzipped my jeans releasing my engorged member. I was hard as a rock and she was as wet as a stream as I positioned myself for entry. With one steady thrust, her moist, wet cavern swallowed my manhood hungrily. She let out a continuous moan as I pulled out and plunged inside of her, two times, three times, then four times. Her wetness engulfed me, wrapping my dick in a murderous grasp. My body tingled, and the top of my head began to itch. As I thrust my fifth and final time, I shouted out victoriously and released a torrent of semen deep inside her. Immediately my body went limp and lifeless. I rested my head on her shoulder. Inside of our heaving chests our two hearts beat as one.

We sat there silently soaking in the epic grandeur of the moment. For once I was a complete and happy man. All of life's problems disappeared into oblivion. The smell of victory filled the air and it was sweet. Peace had truly befallen me. All of my life I had waited to find true happiness, and finally it was right in front of me.

I turned and gazed into Lorena's eyes, "I love you Lorena. You are the best thing that has ever happened to me. I want to be good and take care of you from here on out. I think you are amazing. How does that sound to you?"

"John, I love you too," she replied, in her thick Spanish accent.

Then in a blinding flash all of the kitchen lights

turned on with a flick! We heard the hum of the fluorescents as they quickly illuminated. My eyes crossed as my eardrums were assaulted from a silhouette in the doorway.

"What the hell is going on in here?" screamed Janet.

Chapter 7

Beyond the horizon lies your future, but it is up to you to step forth and embrace it. While you may not always like where you are standing, it is only you who put you there. Sometimes in life you can learn by witnessing destructive behavior, treating people poorly, or even from something traumatic, but a key component of the human condition is to grow through experience. Friends and enemies will come and go, but knowledge will stay with you forever. As a result of my own misdeeds, I am trapped in a dark dismal place. I need to get free and ride into the sunset. What will take me far from here? Am I even worthy of it? These are the questions I toil over daily.

I suppose I could say fuck the world and liberate my mind. It is a rather conflicting situation that I am left to pursue: how does one take accountability for one's thoughts, actions, or his sins? Do you stand atop the roof screaming, "Fuck, I did this shit! And now I am so sorry for it!" My poor choices have plagued my entire existence. Please forgive me world for I did not know what I was doing. I was a weak, fragile mind, and now my regrets have me facing an insurmountable task.

I cannot put my finger on exactly what will justify me and provide me with peace. All I do know is that I am covered with the slime of sanctimonious bullshit. Are you surprised about my candor? What else can I say? I probably am not even worthy of redemption anyhow…are you? Sometimes in life you just need to confess your wrong doings and let the chips fall where they may. I hope mine land on forgiveness, because I sure could use it. We all want God to forgive us when we stand before him, so we need to start with one another.

True forgiveness begins with love and never ends. True forgiveness forgets any remnants of the deed. True forgiveness releases all memory, never to bring it up again. It is formed in love all the way until the end. Do not forget that you too will need forgiveness from someone one day. Mistakes are a part of life, but hey, I am just the guy who got his dick chopped off, what the hell do I know?

Lorena and I dated for the next several months. About the time we hit the nine month mark, we decided to get engaged. Things were great. She was happy and so was I. We had sex everywhere we were able too. Once we even did it in a Burger King bathroom (and later that night we went out and did 'The Humpty Dance'). We would have sex in parking lots, movie theaters, just about anywhere we went. It was without a doubt, the happiest time of my life. As you know, there had not been many, so I anticipated failure somewhere in my foreseeable future.

If I may say so, looking back on the day of our wedding, I made a devilishly handsome groom. Not to sound conceited, but I was a Marine through and through. I was dressed up in my uniform, and I appeared as polished as the blade on my saber. Rest assured however, that the polished façade on me was just like the one on my saber, strictly for show. I was about to crumble for sure!

Lorena and I had a small ceremony on June 18, 1989. There is not much to say about it because it is of little importance who attended, yet the events that followed had massive repercussions. We then went back to Niagara Falls to have a little party with my brothers and family. Again, it was small, but intimate. Our blissful existence lasted right up until our wedding. Yes, only up *until* our wedding. Enter Tim.

My brother Tim had a serious bout with addiction

and all of its demons. Theft, jail, dependency, Tim was rocking them all. His life was quickly careening out of control. Lorena and I attempted to intervene and be his safety net. We failed miserably. I can directly trace this to the immediate dissolving of our Shangri-La like fairytale romance. We, or should I say, I, asked Tim to move back with us to Virginia and escape his doomed life in Western New York. He gladly accepted the invitation, and inevitably I signed our death certificate. We were finished before we ever had even a chance to begin. It is a crying shame when I think about it. Lorena was my wife, but I chose my brother instead. I made a mistake. I regret that I needed to travel so much further down the road to see the error in my ways.

Back in Virginia, in our one bedroom apartment, Tim hit the streets running. Cocaine, pills, and heroin, wormed their way into our lives via Tim. The drugs lied, cheated, and stole their way into my home, into my brand new marriage. Tim had no reverence to our concerns. He was completely self-absorbed, and that was that… my life, my love, in no way accounted into his thinking.

I have learned that Drugs are like the devil himself!

People will forgo all relationships for the next sweet taste of the noxious mixture. Smoking opium is called, "Chasing the dragon." Smoking cocaine is called, "Riding the lightning." And shooting heroin is called, "Dancing with the devil." All for good reason, because you're heading south of heaven the entire way! No one escapes the clutches of addiction unscarred. Some people manage to skirt by, but everyone experiences loss from it. Drugs never propel you forward. At first they just thrust you sideways through different realms. Then, once they grab hold, they take you on a savage downward spiral, eventually leading to your demise, and all of this long before your time has come. It is sad. I have seen drugs take so many before they have the chance to reach their full potential.

Tim was in the throes of full-on addiction. In addition to the drugs, he drank too much. He was a complete mess and he did not care. It is difficult for people to break bad habits and Tim had no intention of breaking his, but because of his loyalty to me as a child, I felt obligated to stand beside him. It was this decision that ruined my marriage. As much as I loved Lorena, she was an outsider to my childhood misery, and Tim as you know, was an insider. He stood by me through all of the pain that I endured as a child. We were forced to watch one another be penetrated by that monster. He never told anyone about it either… that is loyalty.

Tim's loyalty to me and mine to him, superseded my devotion to Lorena, and it was here my transformation began. I do not know how things spiraled out of control so quickly. Lorena hated that Tim shared our tiny apartment, and for good reason. He was privy to any and all of our dealings. If we had sex, Tim knew, if we fought, he knew that too. We had zero privacy. Everything began to unravel. Lorena would bitch about Tim constantly. The incessant complaining drove me to seek relief. I chose alcohol… probably a poor choice.

This next portion I am about to cover will most likely disgust you. If it does not… you might want to get your head checked. No one truly knows what it is like to be me, but I will try to clarify. With empty dreams, a heavy conscience, clenched fists, and feelings that only I know, my heart weeps. I will do my best to explain the monster that I was and the torment that ensued for Lorena. Along with Tim's drug use came my drinking. Along with my drinking came Lorena's bitching. Along with Lorena's bitching came my spousal abuse, and it came in spades!

I never had one of those lives where good things just arrived on my doorstep. I wanted to find true happiness and for me, it was not in Niagara Falls, which is why I joined the Marines. I knew there was a better life out there than I had at home. I decided to walk the earth and find my stride. The road you are on is chosen by you, so I went out to find peace. After I was molested, everything, and everyone in my life was kept at a distance. I did not want to feel the pain and torment of abuse anymore. I did not allow people to get close enough to hurt me again. After all that I had endured, it turns out I became the monster that I had so desperately tried to escape from. I became the abuser.

There is an elementary philosophy that states, those who have been abused, will abuse in the future. Well, call me cliché from here on out because I did just that. I am going to try to be as open and honest as I can about my demonic transformation into the Husband from Hell. I am doing this in the hope of sparing others from going down the same road and experiencing this tragedy. I hope my honesty and candor help at least one. It is a sad tale of woe, but here goes.

While Tim was drugging, I began drinking. I had always drunk before, but when Tim moved in Lorena's bitching became incessant, so I coped with alcohol. I began to consume it in mass quantities. The more I drank, the more blurry the lines of decent human behavior became.

At first it began with verbal tirades. We would fight back and forth while Tim just sat there high. I would always defend him no matter how wrong he was. Lorena's Latin flare erupted daily. She would rant in half Spanish and half English so I only knew a portion of what she was saying, and in my drunken state this only further infuriated me. She would yell all day long. I would beg her to stop, when that did not work, arguments ensued.

What was so crazy about this insane dissemination of our relationship was that we attacked one another like bitter rivals. Unlike two people who were so in love only a few weeks before, we insulted, threatened, and treated one another as if we despised each other's very existence. Our disdain for each other escalated. There was no honeymoon bliss for us. We went straight from, "I do," to "I hate you!"

My brother Bill came to visit for a weekend when he was passing through Virginia on one of his trips around the country. Tim, Bill, and I began having drinks to celebrate our reunion before we went out bar hopping for the night. As we continued drinking, Lorena started complaining. The more we drank, the more she bitched. She and I started hurling insults back and forth. Things were escalating to a dangerous level but we continued flirting with disaster. He said, she said, fuck you, fuck me, it was all being said… and then it happened.

"Fuck you faggot!" Lorena screamed at me from the kitchen into the living room.

Instantly my mind exploded! I was brought back to the place where I was savagely abused by that depraved sodomite. I remembered him whispering to me while he would fuck me, "You like that don't you faggot?"

Visions of rape, sodomy, and torment instantaneously filled my head! Anger and rage coursed through me like an errant locomotive! I saw red, and I lost complete control! I sprang off the couch from in between Tim and Bill. I ran into the kitchen, and slapped Lorena as hard as I could. Bouncing helplessly, she flew across the floor like a bottle cap discarded from a speeding car's window. She ended up in a crumpled mess on the floor alongside the stove. Oh mercy, that was not abominable enough for my enraged anger, so I ran over to her and followed it up with a kick to the stomach. Lorena screamed out in pain. In a flash Bill and Tim grabbed me, and dragged me back into the living room.

It was only a matter of moments when there was a boisterous knock at my door. "Complex Security," was announced from the hallway.

Tim opened the door and in stepped some minimum wage clown with an inferiority complex. "I have had complaints of loud noise and arguing. Can you please keep it down so I don't have to come back?"

"Yes sir," we said just to placate his minimal authority. He did not even see Lorena. My first case of domestic violence had slipped through the cracks of legality. If I were caught and arrested on that first episode, I might never have done it again. But I was not caught, so I continued.

It followed the same scenario time after time.

Lorena and I would fight, it would escalate, I would hit her, and in the morning I would apologize. And while this did not happen every day, it did happen pretty regularly. We were oil and water when I drank, and I drank often. We were doomed from the start, I just didn't know it yet. One thing that I did know for sure, it looked like Lorena was going to have to start explaining where she kept getting all of the black eyes at the salon.

Chapter 8

What can I say about spousal abuse? Well nothing respectable, that is for sure. Men who hit women must have something seriously wrong with their genetic makeup. One of the wires in their heads is either not attached or crossed in some way. There are certain things that every person has to have in order to be a sane, contributing, member of society. At this point in my life, I was neither sane nor contributing. The cold grim reality is that I was a scumbag, all the way down to my ugly core.

The truth rarely looks good on anyone. Most people just hide their flaws remarkably well. I am telling all in this book in hopes of sparing others from the horror of my personal experience. One thing I have come to know is that what hope gives, the truth takes away.

Constant beatings from a drunken husband were partially the result of Tim's extended visit. Lorena received more than her share of beatings in our marriage. I drank too much. Add to that I was a terrible person, and your recipe for disaster is complete. She experienced torment of epic proportion.

Tim's drug addiction was as out of control as I was. He drank and drugged every day, and I followed suit with my drinking. I tried to keep up with him, and Lorena tried to stop us both. Since I was drunk every night, I woke up hung over and miserable every morning. This did not bode well for my young bride. Our marriage went from fairytale to nightmare in an instant, and I was the evil king.

We began to argue more and more. Some days, it never stopped. Our fights started over little things and slowly over time escalated to allegations of infidelity. Lorena's jealousy was out of control, but truthfully, I think it made our sex even hotter.

Despite our vicious fights, Lorena and I had sex all the time. I was a greedy lover though, so she rarely climaxed. I would love to puff my chest out and tell tales of my sexual prowess, but they would be fabricated. I said I was coming clean and telling all in this book, no matter how it made me look. So here we go. I was a premature ejaculator, and if there were more than two minutes of actual penetration, I was setting a new record.

I do not know exactly how my maddening descent

into depravity began. Part of it was the alcohol, and part of it was Lorena's bitching, but it was my mostly my military training pushing me over the edge. My training had given me a god complex. A *god complex* is when you think and feel so powerful, that you try to control all of those around you. Feeling all mighty around Lorena, I began to flex a different kind of muscle. I suppose a key contributing factor also was the sexual abuse that I had suffered as a boy. I had a deep seeded longing to qualify my childhood abuse in some sick way. Years of counseling have left me still unsure why someone would need to control another. I have said previously, those who have been abused will one day become the abuser.

The first time I decided to impose my will on Lorena went like this. We were arguing about whatever situation had her Latin feathers ruffled. She called me a faggot, because she knew it infuriated me. Tim was out somewhere probably getting drugs, and we went at it tooth and nail.

"Fuck you Lorena, Tim's not going anywhere! He's staying with us until he gets himself straightened out. If you don't like it, take your immigrant ass back over the border!" I screamed across the room.

In her thick Spanish accent she replied, "Oh no, mister man want to suck Tim's dick like a little faggot!"

Once again, I sprang up and made a mad dash across the room toward her. Once I got close enough, I let her have it. SMACK-- right across her mouth! But this time something was different. This time, I did not kick her or slap her again. This time, almost through an out of body experience, I wanted to shame her. I wanted her to feel what it was like when I was a boy. I wanted her to know just how wrong it all was, how after this, she would never call me a faggot again. This time, she would bleed for her insult.

I thrust her down onto the floor and began tearing away at the flimsy garments she was wearing. I shredded off her clothes in an instant, exposing her tiny vulnerable backside. She cried out, but it fell on deaf ears. I stripped her down right there on the floor. The fluorescent kitchen light shone my evil reflection on her ass cheeks. I was a man possessed. Once she was naked before me, I attacked her like a grizzly bear. She tried writhing and wiggling to escape, but I had her from behind, and so my military training easily bested her. The physicality of me controlling her had my dick rock hard. I knew I wanted to punish her tiny body. I was going to hurt her for the repeated insults of the rape I endured as a child. I knew there was only one way she would fully understand and comprehend what I had felt. So I did what was done to me.

With her nude body before me, I laid my weight onto her and mercilessly thrust my rock hard cock into her anal cavity. With one fatal swoop, I buried all of my manhood up to my pelvis. The tearing sound or her anus was muffled only by the horror of her screams. She continually cried out in pain as I savagely thrust my engorged member inside her. The more she cried and begged, the more vicious I became. Her pain was my sustenance. I continued pumping in and out as she went into a raging frenzy. I viciously served Lorena degradation and humiliation courtesy of my anal assault.

I continued pumping in and out of her until finally, the tight, blood soaked stimulation of her asshole unleashed a torrent of my demon seed deep inside of her. I finished with two final stiff pumps. Then I rolled off of her. She curled up in a ball and began to cry.

I arose and looked down at her disheveled heaving body, "Who's the faggot now you fucking cunt?"

Chapter 9

Our dissemination into domestic violence had begun with my growing aversion to Lorena's wise-cracking mouth, but perhaps the real elephant in the room was the fact I had no idea how to wrap my fragile mind around the military training I had received, and meanwhile carry on in everyday life. I could not control my emotions. I was already full of anger and fear, and now I was primed and ready to go off at a moment's notice... all of the things the Marines had taught me to be. My combat-ready mind was incapable of dealing one on one with Lorena, hence the forced sex and shaming. I was a time bomb ticking. My fuse was short, and it was lit. Sometimes I sit and wonder if my real demon in all of this was the United States Military? After all of the years gone by, I am still not sure. I am a true product of my environment. Life is difficult enough when you start out poor, uneducated, and victimized. That is why I am trying to make right by admitting all of my wrongs. Maybe I can help someone to be a better person, or maybe I can stop someone's abuse; I can only hope that my words might be valuable to some.

Regardless of where I place the blame for my disgusting character and immense perversion, it would only be a matter of time until karma would come looking for payback. You can only kick a dog so many times before it is going to bite you. Not that I am referring to Lorena as a dog in any way, but I think she got her payback tenfold, and man did that shit hurt!

Tim eventually moved back to New York. Still battling his addictions to this day, nothing has changed in his world. Most likely, he will end up like ninety-nine percent of all junkies on the planet: dead long before his time. I wish that this was not the case and that he could finally get his life straight, but that is probably not going to happen.

You would think that with Tim out of the picture, Lorena and I would now be better off. What really happened is that her true nightmare began. No wonder we made headlines. Our relationship, our marriage, was toxic. Beyond the alcohol, I was now addicted to the craziness and the violence. I was a monster. I would hit her whenever she got lippy. Over the next couple of years, we had horrible fights, but we always made up. It seemed to me that she loved to provoke me. When the forced sex took place it was usually instigated by her calling me a faggot. I cannot help but wonder if Lorena got off on it in some sick way. I feel I cannot take full responsibility for all of our madness; but I will settle on ninety-nine percent. It was weird... sometimes I wanted to kill her, and sometimes I just wanted to love her. I failed at both.

I started taking on odd jobs to help supplement my meager military income. Because of my physical attributes, bouncing at local bars was a natural fit. I had become a major fan of alcohol since Tim's arrival, and I continued my support long after his departure. Not to mention, I got free drinks to work the door so it made being a drunk much easier. When you are a drunken, wife beating, asshole, it usually helps if you get your drinks for free.

So that is how the next few years went for Lorena and me. We rarely spent quality time together. In the afternoon I would nap after work, and then close the bar at night. The nights were lonely for her. It was simply a marriage of convenience after the first year, which fit into Lorena's quest for citizenship and so at the time, I felt no guilt whatsoever.

Lorena needed to be married to a United States citizen for five years in order to become a legal citizen herself. It became obvious she would put up with just about anything. Since I was already a woman beating, drunkard, rapist, husband, I figured, why not be a philanderer as well? Because of my staggering physicality and modest good looks, picking up women at work was easy. I did not have to do anything, and on nights when I would toss someone out, sex was guaranteed. I am not exactly sure why, but I think women get aroused when men fight over them. For example, one night after fighting two drunken customers in the parking lot, the girl involved dragged me into the ladies' room and sucked my dick like a mother-fucking vacuum. I considered this just a perk of the job. Let us be honest, not many men can, or would, say no to a blow-job. I certainly know I couldn't… and didn't.

Remember, I was a Marine: young, dumb, and full of cum. At the end of the night, I would take my dirty dick back home and climb into bed alongside Lorena. Yup, I really was the ultimate asshole.

Chapter 10

With all of my late night indiscretions taking precedence over my marriage, it was doomed to fail. But who knew I would fail with such epic grandiosity on the worldwide stage? I mean really? I literally fucked up holy matrimony so badly, that my name exploded all over the media. I was immediately known the world over as a scumbag.

Since the event, the last twenty years of my life have been ridiculous. There were many days that I felt like giving up. With all that I have experienced, I just know there has to be a lesson in this for someone out there. Otherwise, what was the point of all of this?

The torment that I have endured is way beyond ugly, but I have brought it upon myself. I have chosen to tell all in this book, not in an attempt to win a Man of the Year Award, but to gain forgiveness. I believe that once a man has admitted his fault publicly before his peers, he should be forgiven for all wrong doing. I hope that the world can forgive me as readily as they hope that God will one day forgive them. That is the best I can hope for, a fair shake. I guess I will have to wait and see just how everyone takes this. I have my fingers crossed.

Back to my marriage: each day that Lorena and I spent together was worse than the one preceding it. Constant bickering between us usually resulted in some form of physical violence; it was just commonplace in our life. I hate to admit it, but we fought like drunks in a bar. If we argued, it usually ended in fisticuffs. Regularly, Lorena was the first to throw punches because of her Latin temper. I followed suit if restraint did not work. What else could I do?

Our fights were volatile. Emotionally scarring words were thrown at each other, violent assaults took place, and at times, even blood was shed. Lorena would haul off and strike me with whatever she could get in her hands. She even rang my bell with a frying pan on several occasions, as it was her favorite weapon of choice. She accused me daily of infidelity, and more often than not, she was right.

Throughout the process of writing this book, this time of reflection has shown me just how despicable I was. Maybe I still am a despicable creature? I could fill hundreds of pages telling how I was the worst husband there has ever been, but this next yarn should suffice.

It was midsummer of our second year together when Lorena and I were taking a weekend getaway. We had just packed up the car with our suitcases when we started bickering back and forth. The reason for the feud escapes me now, but at the time, it seemed like the world was coming to an end. We were just getting into the car when our fight escalated to a fever pitch. We had not even pulled out of the driveway when we went at it full-on.

Nothing was sacred as the insults were flying. "Fuck you faggot! You like having your ass fucked don't you John?" Then she punched me in the face.

It was on! She badgered me, so I battered her right there on the front seat. I punched her so hard that her head bounced off of the passenger side window. The smacking sound of my fist against her face resonated through the air. A hollow thud followed when her head hit the window. Then she let out a loud, pain filled whimper. The misery inside the car was palpable. I was completely out of my mind. It was like the devil himself had taken control of me.

The air smelled of blood from the cut above her eye I had just inflicted. As I continued to fill with rage, her face continued to swell. It was time for me to show her who was the boss. And this time, when it was over, she would remember the boss was me!

In her discombobulated state she was incapable of defending herself, and I took full advantage. "You fucking bitch!" I screamed as I pounced on her like a cheetah on a weakened antelope. I began choking her with both hands as I let loose with a verbal tirade of obscenities. "You fucking, no good, immigrant cunt, I hope you die!" I yelled at the top of my lungs as she gasped helplessly. I continued my vocal and physical onslaught, as she began to turn blue from asphyxiation.

I don't know exactly what caused my plummet into perversion and abuse, but I could not control myself. I was simply a man possessed. The more she lamented, the more my bloodlust grew. I let go of her throat, only long enough to shred off every stitch of her clothing and pull down my pants. She spit into my face which only furthered my excitement. My dick became as hard as granite in the mêlée. She was clawing and scratching for her life from beneath me. The intense stimulation of her struggle bombarded my brain with arousal. Like a frothing dog lost in momentary insanity, I satisfied my malicious needs as I thrust my engorged cock inside of her clenched vagina. She let out a horrible scream.

With each penetration I devoured her soul like a piece of chocolate cake. I dug deeper into degradation with each pelvic thrust. I tortured her as much as I possibly could.

When it was over, I just clambered off of her and went into the house. She on the other hand, was left violated on the front seat of our shitty car. See, I told you I was the worst husband there ever was. Lorena was simply a casualty of my depravity, and now she was, forever scarred.

Chapter 11

Things were way beyond dysfunctional in 'Bobbitt-Ville.' If our marriage was terrible after one year, then after two, it blew monkey balls. It was downright disgusting. For the next couple of years I banged random women at work whenever the opportunity presented itself. When I came home drunk in the morning, I would abuse Lorena if I felt like it. If I didn't, I wouldn't. Not every day or night, but frequently enough that it was way too much.

By year three I should have known that my dick was getting cut off. What can I say? I was and still am a complete piece of shit. I still to this day attempt to justify my total physical domination of Lorena as her acceptance of my sexual advances. Not like she even had a choice, because if I wanted to fuck, we fucked. I was so deranged that I defended my disgusting deeds by claiming it aroused her.

I would terrorize her daily, yet I wonder why she tried to kill me. But if this tale of woe in some way helps to stop just one battered woman from being abused, than the writer of this story has done his job.

Rape, rape, and more rape, that is what Lorena got, but as I said, not every day, just regularly. In my own defense, she could have left, or even worse, went to the law. And speaking of the law, now let me illustrate just how flawed our system is. It will just take this portion of our story for you to see just how alone a battered woman can be.

At the four year mark, Lorena finally got tired of all the bullshit and told me she was moving out. My pride told me this was going to get ugly, far uglier than our usual nastiness. She was going to pay for leaving me, and I was going to see to it. I would screw her, (both literally and figuratively) before she could screw me.

So in my regular form, I attacked her and forced her to submit to me sexually. To both degrade and infuriate her, I whispered names of women I had been fucking in her ear. She cried and whimpered as I thrust myself inside of her. Her pain was an aphrodisiac for me. The more she lamented the more engorged my cock became. Her tears only stimulated my shameful desires further as I drove myself in deeper and deeper. I felt her wither into her shattered soul and I left her defeated in a crumpled mass of disgrace. I left her where she lay.

She spent the rest of the night in our bedroom crying hysterically. Meanwhile, I made a secret phone call to have a friend to come and help me move out the next day. I slept on the couch that night. The next morning Lorena snuck out of the apartment before I awoke. I did not know it at the time, but the next morning on her way to work, she went to the police station and attempted to file a restraining order against me. Because of the time involved to file the petition, she realized in order to avoid being late for work, she would have to return and try again in a few days. Due to the lengthy process, Lorena did not receive the help that she so desperately needed. I would have to say that is one epic fail by our judicial system.

Meanwhile, after work that same day we both ended up back at the house. We walked around in complete silence as we attempted to mask our disdain for one another. A knock at the door broke the silence: it was my friend Bobby.

Lorena snapped! "What the fuck is he doing here, John?"

"He is going to help me move out tomorrow morning," I shouted back tauntingly.

"But I told you that I was leaving John!" She was furious!

"Well, now we are both leaving bitch! I'll bet I'm packed and gone before you! I will see you later cunt."

I signaled for Bobby to follow me out of the apartment. I informed him, "We can move my things out tomorrow morning while Lorena is at work. Now let's go get some drinks and celebrate my newfound freedom!"

I was sad but I did not see any point it carrying on about it. That certainly was not going to fix anything. It was just one more thing that I experienced in my life that was not going to work out for me. Fuck it, what could I do?

Bobby and I went out drinking for the night. As boys do, we got drunk, closed the bar, and then went to breakfast. When we returned to the apartment, Lorena was fast asleep. I set Bobby up on the couch with a pillow and blanket. After bidding him good night, I went into our bedroom. Being a most notable scumbag of despicable degree, I was not going to let our last night together pass without incident.

I looked down upon Lorena's sleeping body through intoxicated eyes. It was time to climb aboard the Ecuadorian Express. (That is what I jokingly called it when I would force myself upon her.) In my drunken state I believed she loved it! I was completely deluded and out of my fucking mind. I saw her as nothing more than a device solely for my pleasure. A filthy, cock loving slut lay before me, and I was going to show her pain. In my inebriated mind, she wanted it. She wanted it because she always wanted it, and tonight I would deliver it! I pulled the covers back and jumped on top of Lorena. When she woke screaming I slapped her lying cock sucking mouth! This whore was getting what she deserved. I yanked down her panties and began to forcefully fondle her pussy. Yeah, this was how she liked it! I began poking and prodding at her vagina with one hand, as I held her flailing arms at bay with my other. This bitch was getting fucked tonight whether she liked it or not. Do not forget though, in my stupidity, she wanted it. She loved this! All of her screams were just part of our little game. Yeah, she was a filthy cock loving slut, and I was going to treat her accordingly.

    I seized her, and putting of my weight atop of her, thrust my hard cock inside of her. She let out a pained wail. Once again, this was all part of the act. She loved to smell the scent of alcohol on my breath as I forcefully penetrated her while whispering other women's names, and what I had done to them, in her ear. With each pelvic thrust her disintegration into the abyss furthered. Her maddening decent was accompanied by pain and anguish. Don't forget, this was just how she liked it!

    When I finished my final thrust of torment, I rolled off and fell quickly asleep. Her bawling did nothing to wake me. I slept so soundly, in fact, that I did not even notice her get out of our bed. In hindsight that was a mistake, actually, that was just one of my many mistakes. If all of the failures that I have made in my life were straws, and I was a camel, the next one would surely break my fucking back!

Chapter 12

Bad things are almost always perpetrated in secret; that is why ambushes work, because they are done on unsuspecting foes. With that in mind, Lorena stealthily crept from the bedroom, as not to wake me, and into the kitchen. A woman possessed by years of abuse, she returned to the bedroom with a large carving knife in her right hand. Her mind was seething with rage. Like a succubus descending in the night to devour the soul of a weary traveler while he slept, she slithered through the darkness of the bedroom. It was at this precise moment as I lay sleeping, that she chose to claim her retribution. For all of the pain that I had caused her, she would attack the source from which it came, my penis.

Lorena slowly and methodically pulled the covers down below my waist. She studied me for a brief moment as I lay there fast asleep, then she sprang to action. Clutching the knife with murderous intent, she took hold of my penis in a viselike grip with her free hand. With one slice from the sharpened blade and a tug from the other hand, it was done! It was severed! My limp, lifeless dick was no longer connected to my body. My cock was now held in the hand of the woman who despised it more than anything on earth. She had finally exacted her revenge!

It was as if lightning had struck me square in my groin. Bang! I sprang from my slumber and tumbled to the floor in excruciating pain. Lorena hurriedly ran out of the bedroom in a mad dash for freedom with my dick in her hand. I lay in a crumpled, bloody heap, screaming in pain, as she fled never once looking back at me. For me, it was the beginning of the worst of things to come.

Sometimes, I wish that she had cut my throat instead. I lay lost in a hell which no words could describe. There I was, totally alone in agonizing pain, lying on the floor alongside of my bed.

After Lorena severed my penis, I instinctively grabbed hold of the sheet from the bed and used it as a makeshift bandage to cover my gushing groin. I lay there writhing and moaning in misery. Everything was blurry in the shock of the moment.

Then Bobby came running into the bedroom, and his words rang through the morning air like cannon shot. He stood over me, staring down while I held the blood soaked sheet over my midsection. Confused, he screamed, "Holy shit John! What the fuck happened?!"

"Man, I think Lorena cut off my dick!"

As if I had just explained the nuances of quantum physics to a three year old, Bobby responded with a befuddled look on his face, "What?" (How is this shit for a morning wake-up call? No wonder he no longer wants anything to do with me, my story, or my life.)

"You fucking heard me! I think she cut off my cock! Take me to the hospital, NOW!"

Amidst the confusion and the insanity of the moment, Bobby managed to get me out of the house and to the hospital. For his help through all of this, I am forever indebted to him. For his friendship, I will try my best to respect his wishes, and leave him out of this whole debacle. I wish happiness for him and his family. Be well my friend.

When I arrived at the emergency room, the real nightmare began. The nurses could not believe what I told them.

"What seems to be the trouble this morning?" asked the first nurse I saw, seated behind a desk. (I'm pretty sure she was not expecting worldwide news to walk through the door this early in the morning.)

"My wife cut off my dick while I was sleeping!"

"Excuse me sir… she did what?"

"She cut off my cock! I think I'm going to bleed to death! You have to help me!"

"Hold on just a minute sir. Remain calm. Let me take a look," she said as she came around from behind her desk. "I have to remove this sheet to have a look…" Then with one glance she screamed, "DOCTOR!"

The shock and disgust on everyone's face who looked at me that morning told me what I was too scared to see for myself! Karma had come calling, and in the early morning hours of June 23, 1993, it claimed what it was owed. With one malicious flick of Lorena's knife wielding wrist, my personal hell had begun. Feeling like half the man I used to be only hours before, I had been thrown into a quagmire of uncertainty, shame, and humiliation. And to top off my misery, the entire disgusting saga was about to be shown on primetime television around the world. How is that for karma being a motherfucker?

Chapter 13

My already tumultuous life was flipped upside down amidst all of the havoc and confusion on June 23, 1993. Remember, at this exact moment my cock was still lost in a vacant field. I am sorry to let my anger get the best of me here, but that fucking bitch threw my dick out of the window like a piece of chewed up gum, or a smoked cigarette butt. I mean really? I probably deserved something, but emasculation? That is a bit over the top. Then, to throw my cock into a vacant field like yesterday's trash is just wrong! The next portion of my life had me paying for every sin that I had ever committed.

Here is something crucial I feel the need to point out. Through the immense suffering that I experienced in all of this, I paid for my sins against Lorena. Surely my despicable behavior toward her warranted retribution, I do not dispute that, and she got her revenge. Millions of men around the world mistreat women every day, but they do not end up sans their dicks do they? No they do not. So I think having my cock cut off more than makes up for all of my nefarious behavior toward Lorena. Let us not forget, I was left cold and alone, bleeding profusely from my midsection on the floor, the last time that Lorena walked out of our bedroom. I almost died right there in our bedroom. Oh yeah, did I mention that my dick was still in her hand as she made her escape from the horrible scene? It was severed from my body then callously discarded.

Rape and assault cannot go unpunished in civilized society, and they did not in our case; I was emasculated. Then it was all televised globally on primetime for the next straight year. How is that for payback? Can you say Even Steven? I can… that is just about as even as it gets!

After such a meteoric event, everyone on the planet knew the name, John Wayne Bobbitt. I was now the benchmark of how people gauged abuse in relationships. "At least I'm not John Bobbitt," or "Watch out she might pull a Lorena Bobbitt and cut off your dick." Pretty fucked up huh? I was the standard for what not to do, and I was now the punch line to a thousand jokes. What was so terrible, was that I deserved it all.

As I sat alone in my hospital bed upon admission that morning, I fell to pieces. This was a very dark moment. I was plagued with suicidal thoughts. I became jaded as images of my own demise seemed more appealing with each passing moment. I envisioned myself hanging from the rafters dangling on a rope from my broken neck. I imagined plummeting headfirst out of my hospital window until my body exploded below onto the concrete. These thoughts ran rampant through my mind. I wanted to crawl under a rock and die. Lying in my hospital bed, my mind ran amok with torturous thoughts. The very idea of carrying on with life without my penis was brutal. I did not want to live out the remainder of my days as a Eunuch! I wanted to end it all.

Imagine you just had your dick cut off! I had no idea what to do with myself. I was suffering in solitude, and submerged in sorrow. Nothing seemed real except for the misery that surrounded me. One thing became eminently clear in all of this though, I certainly deserved every bit of my pain.

Then, two hours later, I had a glimmer of hope when a doctor walked into my room. "Hello John, my name is Dr. Townshend, I am your urologist. We have found your penis. Dr. Cooper will be performing surgery to reattach it. We will be getting you ready immediately."

When he walked out of the room my mind went into overdrive. A million thoughts raced around in my head colliding with one another. Complete and utter confusion assaulted me. The nurses took me to another room and prepared me for surgery. Once the surgery team was ready, I was brought into the operating room. After being transferred onto the cold, unforgiving operating table, I began to stare at the bright light positioned directly above my head. As a wall of strange masked faces looked down upon me, the anesthesiologist began to count backwards, and I began to cry.

When my eyes opened, the pale fluorescent lighting of the recovery room blinded me temporarily. Immediately, my hands rushed toward my crotch, but the bundle of bandages kept me from any real discovery. The confused look on my face must have said it all because when a nurse walked into my room she said, "The doctor was able to reattach your penis, John. You will have a long road of recovery ahead of you though. Oh, and by the way, they arrested your wife. It has been all over the news."

At that exact moment I felt neither joy nor remorse. My mind was overrun in a narcotic induced blur. I just stared blankly back at her and responded, "Oh, ok… thanks."

I sat slightly elevated in my hospital bed and surfed massive waves of vacuity from the opiate laden pain killers that the hospital was kind enough to provide to me. My mind and body were mushy from the drugs. I was lost in translation, half alive, but mostly dead, swallowed in oblivion.

I remembered thinking to myself, "So this is what Tim is so addicted to. I had better watch myself on this shit, so I don't become an addict as well."

What I did not know before, but became so utterly clear at that moment, was that drugs did not kill pain at all. They simply masked the pain by putting you in a drug-induced stupor. The moment the sweet serenade of narcotics beguile your senses, you are like a goldfish in a bowl. You swim endless circles, drifting aimlessly along in a limbo, never truly accomplishing anything, or reaching a destination.

It is as if the bowl is the drug, and you are the fish. The water is vast nothingness, and the world is just off past the rim of the bowl, but you never quite reach it, or contribute anything to it. You see it from a distance through a hazy film of glass, and no matter how hard you try, you can never get there. As long as drugs course through your veins, you will perpetually wander in obscurity, never realizing your full potential. You become just another wasted life on this earth, another victim of addiction.

After an indeterminate amount of time swimming through the abyss, my doctors walked into the room. I was snapped back to a diluted reality.

"John, we managed to save your penis through both luck and skill. The luck was that the police discovered the other portion of your severed penis within the time constraints we had to successfully reattach it. And the skill, well, that was Dr. Cooper's talented hands. He truly is a masterful surgeon. You have been blessed with a new lease on life because of him."

You would have thought that relief would have washed over me at that moment, but I was so high, I thought $2 + 2 =$ blue. Their words, while I heard them, did not register until later, but when they did... man, was I ever thankful!

(By the way, in case you were wondering, Lorena called 911 after the attack and told investigators where she tossed my cock out of the car. They put out an all-points bulletin and some rookie cop found my severed dick in a vacant field. It was immediately packed it up in ice and sent it to the hospital for the 9½ hour reattachment surgery).

Chapter 14

As I sat alone in my hospital bed, the agonizing pain had me contemplating suicide. In addition, all of the abuse that I had done to Lorena kept replaying like images on a screen. Every tragic event continually played out in my mind: physical abuse, forced sex, verbal tirades, my mind ran the full gamut of all the incidents that had occurred in our marriage. Each vision was more disgusting than the last. I felt in my heart that I deserved to die for my sins.

As fucked up as it all seems, I would not change the events of June 23, 1993, because it brought domestic violence to the forefront of social consciousness. It caused awareness and changed the way the world looked at spousal abuse. Call me a scumbag if you want to, but my tragic incident did more to educate the public to the plight of battered women than anything before or since. So ironically, I guess the hardcore feminists protesting violence across the globe owe me a bit of gratitude now do they not? It sure would be nice to hear rather than a bunch of hateful slander. I am admitting all of this, my deepest darkest secrets, conspicuously, in hopes of stopping future attacks on women.

Once someone commits the act of rape and gets away with it, they will never stop. I know that regular citizens cannot fathom the mindset of a sexual sadist, but I shall try to explain it to you. Rape equals power, but it also equates to a sexual gratification on a different level. When you impose your will on another and force penetration, you become intoxicated by the sudden rush of endorphin packed adrenaline that courses through your veins. This stimulates your mind beyond anything I have ever known. There are no words to describe the euphoric bombardment of your senses. The smattering of violence heightens sexual arousal for some and the experience, though depraved, is orgasmic. It is a warped, demented pleasure, only the most evil could enjoy.

I am told that my gratification from abusing others stems from the horrendous abuse I suffered as a child. Early childhood experiences are the building blocks on which the foundation for adult sexual desires are formed. When a child endures trauma, their psyche can splinter, and a warped sensuality toward pain and degradation may form. This ends up causing deviant sexual desires later in adulthood. Deep rooted perversions are common as most abusive people have some form of abuse in their past. I am not trying to make excuses in any way, I am just citing what I believe.

This may not be a popular topic, but it is a necessary one. People who have been harmed seek to one day become the abuser. It is the simple logistics of cause and effect. When a person is abused, it is like a pebble being thrown in a pond. The initial splash of the pebble landing in the water is the result of the act of the throw. It is the ripples from the initial act that end up reaching out and touching so many. When one life is touched by abuse, it usually ends up touching multiple others, and so on, and so on. A perpetual cycle of abuse begins and carries on for generations. Lorena was kind enough to break my cycle of abuse.

When you take pleasure in the suffering of others, drastic measures must be taken to stop you. It is that simple. By any means necessary, whether by radical rehabilitation, imprisonment, or death, I am in favor of whatever it takes to provide safety for others. It took the slice of a large carving knife to forever alter my way thinking. If it could work for me, it could work for other flawed individuals. Forced castration works!

Fast forward to today. I now live my life with a remarkable woman whom I have never abused, let alone raped, but it took having my cock chopped off for me to see just how wrong I was. This is why I am now a proponent of forced castration. I am the poster boy for rehabilitation through mutilation. As awful as it sounds, it worked for me, and it could work for others. I have never forced myself on another woman since Lorena emasculated me. That is the only way to stop a sexual deviant... you have to chop off their dick. Some people are lucky enough that they can heed the advice of others, but then there are some that can only learn from a lesson paid in blood. I happen to be the latter. It is a sad fact the way society has progressed, but some people need to be made into examples: a deterrent so others see what not to do. My life is now the most normal and satisfying that it has ever been. If I can use my experience to help others, I am happy to do so. If I cannot, please leave me be. I have paid for my crimes in full.

Penile amputation is not as rare as you might think. The phenomenon is rampant in Asian countries. Currently to date there are roughly two hundred men around the world who have had their penises amputated. I however, am one of the only ones to have my penis successfully reattached and in working order without a prosthetic. So, I am a bit of an anomaly, as well as a full-on laughing stock. Now, back to our story.

I felt like shit. Even the optimistic wishes of Dr. Townshend, my urologist, and Dr. Cooper, my reconstructive surgeon, were not enough to cheer me up. The ten hour surgery to reattach my penis was successful, but it was my detached soul that was ailing me. How in the world was I ever going to right all of the wrong that I had done in my life? It was in these moments, alone in the hospital, that it became clear. I needed to get my mind and body right, as well as my soul.

Time lingered in obscurity as I lay alone in my hospital bed. The darkness of my heart left a somberness that I could not escape. The air in my room seemed too stagnant to breathe because I sullied everything around me. I tarnished all that I came in contact with.

After three weeks, I was sent home to heal. Bobby was kind enough to come and stay with me. It was difficult being same apartment where only a few short weeks before the deed had transpired. How is that for a constant reminder of the trauma? Spending every waking moment at the exact place where my penis was severed proved to be counteractive. My body was deprived of true restful healing because of a constant barrage of distressing memories. This torment was debilitating and in addition, I hated the man that I had become.

I am allowing you to delve into the mind of a deviant. Through my candor there is the potential for this book to triumph over spousal abuse, even though I want to blame everyone else for my problems. I, like most of society, am a duplicitous and scandalous individual who has trouble with real change.

To quote the late great Frank Zappa, "Do you know what you are? You are what you is. You is what you am, and a cow don't make ham."

Chapter 15

My life almost ended on the night of June 23, 1993; sometimes I wished it had. Since it did not, however, I faced the long road to recovery (which, by the way, was excruciatingly painful). Relearning many of the rudimentary aspects of life was just pitiful. I could not even take a piss without a catheter for months. When they removed the catheter, I had to learn how to go to the bathroom all over again! With constant agonizing pain running throughout my body, and paralyzing guilt bombarding my mind, all of my days sucked from morning until night. Just one troublesome event after another.

Then the wonderful world of the judicial system joined in and terrible just got way worse! As if I did not have enough trouble on my hands trying to learn to go to the bathroom all over again, now I had reporters crawling up my ass at every turn. I was charged with malicious assault by the prosecutor's office because, in the state of Virginia, a husband cannot be charged with raping his wife if they live together under the same roof. How fucked up is that?

The trial date was set, and my lawyer suggested I lay low from all of the media hype for a while. He sent me to a cattle ranch in Callahan, Colorado, for a month before it began. He may as well have sent me to rancho-kook-a-munga, because I did not see anyone the entire time I was there. With all that was transpiring in the media though, my newfound anonymity was appreciated.

After a month had passed, I returned to Virginia and my trial began. When I arrived for the first day, it was insane. News media from across the country and hoards of angry protesters littered the lawn. Extremist feminists screamed for my head as I ascended the steps of the courthouse. They were even selling novelty t-shirts that read, "Manassas Virginia, A Cut above the Rest." It was a circus, and I was live on the main stage. Fake, bloody, severed dicks were waved, accompanied by slogans of hate. It was a disgusting display of man's inhumanity to man, to say the least. Just a bunch of hate mongers, hating on me, broadcasted live for the world to see.

Inside the courtroom, the theatrics rivaled the spectacle out on the front lawn. Streams of witnesses were paraded to the stand. Some told the truth, and some spewed untruths. It was a sea of misinformation. My trump card however, was the inept prosecution. The district attorney had a hundred fastballs down the middle to knock out of the park, (actually to knock my ass into the penitentiary), but that bozo whiffed every time. Seriously, I think that the prosecutor must have received his law degree by mailing in twenty proofs of purchase to Honey Comb Cereal.

After all of my bullshit and lies, I was eventually found not guilty. What blows me away though, is that I was as guilty as hell, yet I walked. For whatever reason, either sympathy for my emasculation, or a fumbled ball by the prosecution, I was set free. I appreciated that.

Since they were unable to convict me, the district attorney's office then went after Lorena. They were so embarrassed by my trial that they just wanted someone found guilty. There was a two month lull and back to court we went, complete with all of the mayhem. Horror story after horror story was told, yet once again, no one was found guilty. An enormous amount of tax payer money was wasted, and our dysfunction was televised to the world. The best efforts of the district attorney's office only resulted in Lorena having to spend a few days in a mental hospital. For all of the publicity that the case garnered, the end result for me was that I was offered an adult movie contract. Apparently people all over the world wanted to see if my dick would really work or not. So with the trial came my first adult film role, taxpayer money well spent I say. My porn career was indirectly started by the Virginia judicial system. They started out trying to fuck me, and ended up, getting me laid

So here's what happened next: Lorena was launched into feminist superstardom, and I dove headfirst into a world of wild parties, booze, and fast women. It was hard for me to understand all that was going on, since my cognitive skills have always been a bit suspect, to say the least. Only one year since the mutilation of my genitalia, I was under the assumption that fame and fortune awaited me as an adult superstar! Oh yeah, me and my fucked up freak cock were going to get paid!

I had just spent the last four years of my life torturing Lorena with the very cock that she so angrily severed, and now I thought that this was my vehicle to superstardom. Are you kidding me? There must be rats in a laboratory maze chasing cheese that are smarter than I. (I think I just heard the short bus honk outside.)

I am just like Popeye the Sailor-man, "I yam what I yam, and that's all that I am."

At my trial, some fellow Marines testified that I told them that I liked forced sex and making women bleed. I of course, denied it at the trial, but I must have said that. Being braggadocios is foolish in any setting, but to think that it is cool to hurt a woman, well that is just plain idiotic.

You may think my plea for redemption is just a bunch of malarkey, but it surely does take a sincere heart to admit openly to forced sex, sodomy, and physical abuse. In my mind though, I cannot help to think that I too am a victim. After twenty years, I still feel compelled to say that I was wronged. Nevertheless, is a monster like me even worthy of redemption? No matter how shitty a person is, even the worst of us want their life to mean something in the end, and I am no different. Part of me wants to believe I have changed, and part of me just knows I am still the same asshole that I have always been deep down inside.

Chapter 16

In order to be great, a man must boldly face the world alone. On his lonesome journey, he will encounter hoards of opposition as he questions authority, disproves stereo types, and offends the everyman. He must have the courage to accept a life of solitude, and the strength to face it. If he holds true, never conceding his beliefs, he will be heralded, he will triumph in the end. Always live life on your own terms.

Upon conclusion of the trial, I started receiving appearance offers from around the country. Everyone wanted to meet the famed, wife beating rapist who got away with it. After the creation of my band, The Severed Parts, did not rise to the fame and fortune I had hoped for, a famous shock-jock radio show host took me under his wing, and even hosted a farcical telethon to help pay my legal and medical bills. It was part joke, and part real, but it was all pathetic. In my mind, however, I thought that finally I was a real somebody.

In addition, I secured a high powered seedy agent who started booking me day and night. This guy hawked me everywhere that he could. My agent was the epitome of a scandalous scumbag, so we paired nicely. Do not worry about me living the good life off of my media celebrity though. Karma would eventually arrive, and my high powered agent ended up swindling me out of every penny of revenue that I made. How is that for justice? But we will cover all of that soon enough.

I started meeting a variety of different people. My porn career got its start one night while I was attending a Wet & Wild party at a very famous mansion (that shall remain nameless). A certain pornography legend asked me to make a cameo appearance in one of his upcoming films. The Hedgehog, as he is known in the industry, soon changed his plans for me from a brief glimpse in his movie, to a starring role in a feature film. What guy could say no to that? All the nasty slut pussy that I could shake my severed dick at and I did not even have to rape anyone. I was in heaven, or hell, depending on how you looked at it. I decided that I would search for my personal bliss deep inside the anal recesses of adult film actresses. Really, I mean, who knew that you wouldn't find happiness in a den of iniquity?

Party after party, and late night after late night, my life started becoming a blur. I went back to drinking full time. What was truly pitiful was that almost every man and woman I met insisted on seeing my mutilated member. Some wanted to suck it, others wanted to fuck it, but everyone wanted to gawk at it. When I would pull it out people would yelp and yawp. It certainly shocked anyone who was privy to catch a glimpse of my mangled meat. No one had ever seen anything like it. It would be, I would be, the life of the party, almost anywhere "we" went.

A deal was finally struck between my agent and the movie people. Then, before I knew it, there I was on a dingy, musty, porn set. The smell of stale sex and shame permeated the air. When these buxom sluts began to parade around on the set in front of me, even my reconstituted cock sprung to attention. This would be my finest hour, or so I thought.

Standing there I realized, just how serendipitous it was that Lorena's emasculation of me, as vicious as it was, had landed me the starring role in a feature adult film. How crazy is it that my ultimate dream, was facilitated by such a nightmare? It turns out that Lorena's heinous act garnered us both a bit of fame.

At one point or another, every man dreams of starring in a porn movie. However, most people do not know what goes on behind the scenes. For starters, almost all of the sex is cut, then reshot, then cut again. The actual fornication is usually only a few minutes long, but it is the use of different camera angles, and some clever editing, that gives the actors the illusion of superhero stamina. They just keep rolling the same footage from different angles. It only appears that the actors are fucking for hours. Next time you watch your favorite adult film, stop jerking off long enough and focus solely on the scene itself. Pay extra close attention to the surroundings. You will see that it is, in fact, a compilation of the same sex scenes shown from different vantage points. Everyone in the industry knows that many a sexual dynamo has been left on the editing room floor.

One thing that I learned right out of the gate was that just about every bit of emotion is faked. The director tells everyone where to move, how to act, and what to say. Few and far between are the times when the actors are actually enjoying themselves. Orgasms for the women are almost always phony, and as for the men, they get most of their stimulation from fluffers. A *fluff*er is a stage hand that is on the set strictly to get the male actors erect, aroused, or close enough to completion that the camera can get a "money shot." It is all just a bunch of fake-ass hoopla really, and people all over the world spend billions of dollars on it just so they can jack off.

As for the actresses starring in these films, it is obvious that some someone in their past touched them inappropriately. They cannot help themselves but as to have as much sex as possible, in a feeble attempt to mask the shame they feel from the abuse suffered as a child. Now toss into the mix a director, who is usually a film school dropout, with a serious taste for one or more different varieties of narcotics. Then to top it all off, add the bottom feeding extras, slithering around the set, and you my friend have one hell of a party.

There is a section in every porno shop to accommodate almost any sexual inclination or fetish. If you can dream it up, there is someone, somewhere, who is willing to make it into a movie. On the flip side of that coin, there are also an array of people who are willing to pay top buck to watch it. It is all one humungous supply and demand conglomerate. Millions of people want it, so a handful of people supply it. It is elementary economics, but enough about the logistics of the pornography industry; let us get to some fucking!

The craziness of the adult film world engulfed me, and I became fixated on sex. Blow jobs, doggie style, and anal sex were all that I thought about, so much in fact, that it literally consumed me. With this bevy of busty beauties sauntering around, my libido was in overdrive. It is not difficult to be aroused when six women are all begging for your cock in the sultriest of voices. Even my half-dead dick was able to respond. Imagine me, a pig, and porn queens all in the same room together. To me, it was a fucking fairy tale… literally.

I was informed that my first scene was a three way with a big breasted blonde and a brunette. When the director shouted, "Action," I hit the ground running. They gave me, as they give all of the men, a Viagra, so my cock was rock hard and standing at attention. As the scene began we had a short dialog. Then, we all began sloppily kissing one another as they worked their way down my ripped body to unleash my fully engorged manhood. As I sprang free from the denim confinement behind the zipper of my jeans, my wrinkled and deformed cock made its first legendary appearance.

People all around the world were talking about the creepiest fuck stick ever to grace the video screen. It was mangled and embarrassing, but these pussy pounded starlets still swallowed it whole. They playfully licked it, lapping their way up and down the shaft. They would suck and swallow my pathetic, shriveled up head in an attempt to further stimulate the viewer.

In true Marine Corp fashion, I adapted and overcame my adversity. I gave it my all, and the three of us awkwardly worked our way through the scene. With the two ladies of certain distinction in a sixty-nine, I positioned myself behind the one on top. With forceful penetration, I continually and savagely thrust until reaching that old familiar fever pitch. Once I felt my sack ready to erupt, I pulled out and released a torrent of my man gravy all over their faces. They playfully licked and lapped away at one another, reveling in a post sex orgasmic hue (fake or real made absolutely no difference to me) as the camera faded to black.

We did several more scenes over the next few days until we had enough raw footage to head to the editing room. This decision to star alongside women of such ill repute did something to further tarnish my already pathetic reputation. (Truthfully, I do not think it had anything to do with the ladies.) I went from a laughing stock, to full-on buffoon in an instant. One thing we learned from all of this, everyone loves to watch the circus freaks.

Chapter 17

People all over the world were talking about the dim-witted psycho starring in a new pornographic movie with his freakish cock. Truly, it was like nothing that had ever graced the screen. Speculation on my guilt or innocence immediately fell to the wayside and became secondary to just how entertaining, yet incredibly appalling, the sight of my mangled member was. It was all anyone was talking about, and it quickly became the fastest selling adult movie in history.

After the release of my first film and its immediate rise to success, another movie was scheduled. This time, I would undergo an augmentation surgery first, hence the movie's title. (In case you are curious as to why I am not directly naming any of the people, places, or things that I make reference to, it is because I am not taking a chance on being. I have been made painfully aware of just how shamefully scandalous people are. Every person that I have ever put faith in has screwed me over. Right down the line, people have raped and stolen everything I have ever held dear. From my innocence to my finances, they have robbed me of it all. So they can all suck a bag of dicks!)

After completion of my augmentative surgery, I needed to allow my new, thicker, and fuller cock time to heal. Then it was back to work! Once again, I indulged to the fullest, satisfying all of my wanton desires. Double header blow jobs, anal, three ways, I did it all. I let my freak flag fly! There is nothing more appealing than a bunch of devilish sluts begging you to fulfill all of your carnal desires. But truth be told, my second porno role went much like the first, full of awkward sex and terrible acting. The only real difference was that I had a new thicker fuller cock to sling around the set. Even flaccid my meat looked much better; it no longer looked like a shriveled up raisin sitting on top of a cucumber anymore.

Regardless of all my rough and tumble talk though, I guess I am a boring romantic at heart. I remember at one point sitting alone on the set thinking just how much I missed the love that Lorena and I once shared: the way the sun would reflect off of her hair, her scent, and the taste of her lips. For one brief instant, I longed for her touch. Sadness filled my heart and tears filled my eyes. I could not help but think of the dreams that we had shared, and all that went so terribly wrong. I heard the distant voices of my broken heart telling me that I should have seen it coming. Then, a big set of titties in my face with a glass of water and a Viagra in her hand snapped me back to the task at hand... yeah buddy, it was time to get laid.

My first scene in my second film was with a red headed starlet. We began to kiss with lips full of passion. The smacking sound resonated across the set as I began to massage her ample breasts. I began to lick and suck at her enormous areola's and nipples as she vigorously rubbed at my crotch. Then I rose to present my bulging groin at chin level as she unleashed my new beast and swallowed me with one effortless gulp. She continued taking my cock deep with bowel shaking sound effects as I pumped my hips. She gave me an evil gaze as she spit on my dick and savagely jerked at it. Then she pulled down her panties and hiked up her skirt as I dropped to my knees. I plunged my tongue deep inside her moist, musty cavern. A twinge of tang assaulted my taste buds as I tried to mask my distain for her odoriferous vagina. She let out a series of fake moans and sighs in a pathetic attempt to simulate stimulation. After the director had enough footage he cued us to switch positions, and that could not have come soon enough. I then plunged my cock, balls-deep inside of her funky smelling vagina. She let out a bogus moan of ecstasy. I began to hurriedly pump in and out as she shouted slutty phrases of encouragement. After switching positions seamlessly from doggie style into reverse cowgirl, she road me hard in her attempt to put me away wet.

"Harder, deeper, faster, oh, fuck me, Frankencock!" She screamed at the top of her lungs

We switched up our tempo on multiple occasions as she pretended to climax multiple times. It all finally culminated in one monstrous extravaganza of simulated euphoria, and the director yelled, "Cut!"

I ended up doing a few more scenes showcasing my newly refurbished nine and a quarter inch penis. While no one was actually impressed, I did my best, and the rest, as they say, is history.

When all was said and done, we did a tour around the country to promote the second film. Hotels, late nights, heavy drinking, and hookers were slated on tap for our excursion. Meet and greets, signings, and parties, it was a revolting hodgepodge of debauchers, fornicators, drunks, and druggies, touring the country pandering filth. If I did not have problems before, I would certainly have a few new ones after spending time with those freaks.

No matter where we ended up, in any city, we were the life of the party. Everyone we met wanted me to whip out my dick, guys and gals alike gasped, gawked, and shuddered, but they all begged to see it.

In all of my travels, in my endless time spent searching for something to make me complete, my broken heart always went back to Lorena. She got the best, and the worst of me... enough said.

Meanwhile, I repeatedly asked my agent when I would start receiving my movie royalties from the films, but there was always an excuse. After a year I figured out why: because there were no royalties coming my way. Now, they were all his royalties. Somehow, someway, amidst all parties and the hubbub, I signed away my share to him. I was handed the keys to the kingdom of wealth, but I squandered my chance by literally losing the keys! Fame, fortune, and everything that goes with it, I had the groundwork for greatness laid at my feet, but I was too foolhardy to grasp it. Yup, I signed away all of my rights to my agent, and I was entitled to nothing. The media announced that I made a million dollars, when in reality, I did not see a dime.

I could have spent the rest of my days living happily ever after off of the royalties from my two adult movies. Instead, I was suddenly broke, destitute, and discarded like yesterday's trash. My agent stopped answering my calls, and my lawyer eventually followed suit. As for me, I was entirely alone.

Because of my inability to comprehend the perplexities of the business world, I was duped out of a small fortune. You can rationalize it anyway you choose, but I believe it was karma. I have an affinity for all of the perpetual losers out there in the world.

"You can't polish a turd."

By the end of my whirlwind porn-star run, my two brothers Bill and Tim, were living in Las Vegas together. When they heard I was penniless, they gave me a call (I imagine right after they had a nice long laugh). They suggested that I come out for a visit. They told me that I could stay with them until I got back on my feet, and so with no other options in my life, I loaded up all of my belongings into my car made the trek to Nevada.

When I finally arrived in Las Vegas, I noticed a large dark cloud that seemed out of place. It hung low, looming ominously over the city as I made my way down the strip. Something told me that I should keep on driving right out of town, but of course I did not. I wish now that I had... it would have saved me three years of my life.

My agent had called with a couple of vain attempts at resurrecting my career, but they all proved fruitless in the end. Twice I was recommended for celebrity boxing and wrestling matches, but none of that ever panned out. There was even a gimmick where I was ordained as a preacher to stir up some controversy, but that just made me even more of a laughing stock.

Then, the famous porn star who hooked me up with my first movie called me with a job opportunity, which I graciously accepted. I took a job as a bartender, greeter, and limo driver, at a certain Ranch up near Reno which provided a safe working environment to ladies of the oldest profession, and not to mention that I would be able to work around easy women... so I liked that! Also, I figured it might give me a chance to work on a bit of comedy in front of the customers as they paraded in and out. You see, I always had hopes and aspirations of being a stand-up comedian, and now that I had the notoriety, I figured it would be as good a time as any to give it a whirl. Customers would arrive, and in order to break the ice, I would throw a joke or two at them. They were usually something in reference to my dick, my dick being chopped off, or my dick ending up somewhere it should not have, so it got old before it even had a chance to start. My comedic attempts were usually met with a laugh or two, but quickly fizzled out after the redundancy wore on peoples nerves.

I have to say the Ranch had its share of strange customers, not to mention the fact that with all of the different personalities of the ladies working there, it was always very interesting. I loved talking to each of the different girls and hearing what they had going on in their lives. This is where I really began to learn of the idiosyncrasies that made women tick. Many of the girls would sit and talk to me for hours in furtherance of helping me understand them. Some wanted to help me heal from all that I had gone through. The kindness they showed me still baffles me to this day. Turns out there really are,

"Hookers with a heart of gold," in the world.

I would drive the ladies places in the limo if they had errands to run. I would take them shopping, to get their hair and nails done, or anywhere they needed to go. Sometimes I would go to pick up customers if the owner asked me to. I did whatever I was asked to do, but I really liked bar tending the best. As I stood behind the bar I was able to interact with the girls and the customers. It always provided me with entertainment if nothing else. As part of my job I listened, and as another part I told them who I was. People were always shocked when they found out I was the famed John Wayne Bobbitt, so it made for interesting conversations and contacts. I suppose the novelty of having a man whose cock was chopped off serving drinks in a brothel was pretty substantial. Either way I enjoyed my time there.

I am sure you are wondering, and yes I dated one of the girls. Dating a prostitute is not for everyone, but it did not seem to bother me. I did not let our working relationship get in the way of our personal relationship. At night my lady would sneak me into her room. Then feelings started to get involved and we made a bullshit effort to run off together. We went and stayed with her mother in Arizona, but after our break up, when I tried to return and get my job back, the owner of the Ranch told me to go fuck myself because I had taken off with one of the girls.

So finding myself once again alone and destitute, I called my brothers back in Vegas and they told me I could come and crash with them. When I arrived at my brothers' apartment we had our typical meet and greet, just like any reunion after an extended hiatus from one another. We hung out, went out, and then passed out. Tim was still a junkie and Bill, well, Bill was a criminal, but I loved them just the same.

I had picked up a job as a mover. I got into the routine of going to work and began trying to assimilate back into regular society. The fact that I have always been so strong was a substantial asset when it came to moving furniture. It was hard on the back but easy on the brain. I liked that I did not have to use any smarts for this gig, and it was a steady paycheck.

Bill and Tim had a motley assortment of the criminal element stopping by their place all of the time. I never paid any of them much attention to any of these people, until one day a guy asked me if I would like to take a trip to go and steal a bunch of new clothes. Well, being as broke as a joke, I decided what the hell? What could possibly go wrong? Well, what went wrong landed me a two and a half year prison term.

Unbeknownst to me, it turned out that there was a sting going down on a group of people who were heavily into clothing theft. By heavy, I mean to the tune of over $150,000.00 worth of clothing theft. We went to a store in Fallon, Nevada, and the people inside told me to take whatever I wanted. It was a free for all. I only went twice, but after the bust, once investigators and prosecutors heard the name John Wayne Bobbitt was involved though, they were not settling for anything short of a conviction. Initially, I ended up with five years' probation, $5,000 in restitution, and 100 community service hours...which was all fine and good until three years later, after breaking my probation, I was sent to prison. I sure hope they wore a condom too, because the state of Nevada fucked me harder than any porn star ever did.

Chapter 18

I think I must have sold my soul to the devil to be in porn, because I was about to start a stint in hell as payback. After a short trial that seemed more about my notoriety than about my crime, I was quickly labeled guilty. I was sent to the Nevada Department of Corrections for rehabilitation. Just so that you are aware, that "rehabilitation" part is meant with the utmost sarcasm because there is no actual rehabilitation in prison. There is just a shitload of sex and violence. It is a funny thing about the sex though… it's definitely not the kind most guys are looking for!

Have you ever been forced to look down the barrel of straight serious? The moment you step through the gates of confinement, societal rules no longer apply. The fantastic gap between the commonalities of free life and doing time is so vast, that regular citizens could never comprehend it. You see things daily that should never be seen by anyone. There are certain people on the inside that should not be there, and then again there are some people inside who should never be allowed out. I will break it down for you with some simple guidelines to surviving in prison.

Imprisonment is not about gangs, it is about race. While dwelling alongside one another, there is little constructive interaction, mostly just plotting the demise of the opposite race. However, when drugs are involved, most inmates will forgo their racial conflicts, and deal cordially with one another until either a discrepancy or a debt is incurred. Then, punishment is swift and severe as examples need to be made.

Incarceration is not about rehabilitation, it is about doing time and that is all. Time is a difficult adversary for any man, far more intimidating than even the biggest of inmates on the yard. Time has the ability to degrade and demoralize a person to the point of insanity. Time will use shame as its enforcer to torture the mind. Your best bet is to forget about the outside world and concentrate fully on the world you are in. Trust me when I say that worrying about things that you have no control over will only increase your sentence.

Time to reflect on the past is a good thing, but solitary moments will force you to try to justify the actions that caused your confinement. This is what went on with me and my crimes against Lorena. It is very difficult when you are locked up with your thoughts, your guilt, and your feelings. This is why suicide attempts are so common on the inside. It is in those instances, that your key to survival is realizing that while you are forced to bend, you are always free to dream. Understand that though society can lock up your physical body, your spirit and mind is yours to do with what you please.

Let your mind roam freely through happy moments in your life and savor every feature. When you think of fond memories, think of every tiny detail, anything less is an exercise in futility. This will not only help pass time but it will remind you of the things that truly matter. It is in those most cherished moments, that you will find peace and they cannot take that away from you. Use the ability to transport yourself to another place in your mind, which will allow you to feel joy. No matter the torment or persecution they levy against you, never allow them to break your spirit. You need to condition your mind so that it transcends the walls that bind you, thus giving you freedom of a different kind that they cannot take away. It is the small battles that prove decisive and allow you to persevere.

Doing time is best done through strict regimens. Cleaning your cell meticulously, exercising vigorously, and studying ravenously, are simple ways to not only better yourself, but they are ways to better cope with the situation. Soul searching is how I found a way to make me a better person.

You need to find out what works for you; and most importantly always be aware of your surroundings. Basically, trust no one who is not of your race and as far as for people of your own ethnicity, only trust them to a certain degree. Do not forget everyone around you is a criminal, and loyalty only goes so far. On the flip side of that coin, friendships and brotherhood can be forged on the inside that supersede anything you have ever experienced in the outside world, but always be skeptical. If you follow these simple guidelines you will most likely make it out alive. Just do yourself a favor and always watch your back.

Violent assaults and sodomy run rampant in the prison subculture as guards turn a blind eye to it. It is a classic example of street justice in its rawest and most primordial form. While it has been proven countless times over the years that court justice can be purchased, street justice on the other hand, has no price. Not to mention that with my sweet ass parading around, coupled with my alleged spousal abuse charges, I would be a target. So I prepared myself for the worst to come. That is really all a man in my situation can do: prepare for the worst and hope for the best.

My first stop was the Clark County Detention Center for an extended ten month layover. Anyone who knows about being locked up knows that county time is the worst time. The reason is that you have everyone, maximum security inmates, nonviolent, and sex offenders, all penned up together. It is just one mixed up hodgepodge of the dregs of society, and they are all expected to coexist. It almost always ends up ugly, as sex offenders, in particular, are always 'green lit.'

To be green lit means that they have a standing T.O.S. order from all gangs, which means, "terminate on sight." You do the math. Fortunately, my Marine Corp training would come in handy. Being the kind of man who would rather die on my feet, than to live on my knees, my mettle and fortitude would surely be tested. I was prepared to defend myself no matter the odds against me.

There is only one positive thing to being caged like an animal. It allows you to slow down and see what is truly important. The fast pace out in the free world moves so quickly that people never embrace the things that really matter. Everyone is far too concerned with the conditions and permissions set forth by society. Once someone has their freedom ripped away, they tend to long for the little things. It is just something that I have come to know from my lengthy imprisonment.

I believe that every person should be forced to do either a year in the military, or a year in prison, that would make the world would be a much better place. Having done time in both, I have learned how to keep my nose out of things that do not concern me. That is one of the worst problems in conventional society: people butting their noses in where they do not belong. That shit will get you killed in either the military or in jail.

Now, back to my term in the Clark County Correctional facility. With my famous name I was immediately put to the test. It seemed as though any young punk who found out who I was wanted to "make their bones" on me. Making your bones is prison slang for earning your stripes. In other words, fighting, proving to everyone you are battle tested and true. That is how you get respect in lock-up. I am sorry, as I did not make the rules, but people will not respect you if you do not fight in prison. It is a superficial bullshit stigma that a propensity for violence is the only way to get a name, and save your own ass... literally. Sometimes even being tough is not enough. If ten guys want to fuck you, I don't care how tough you are, you are getting fucked! It really is all that those kinds of people understand though. Without being willing to fight, you will find yourself forced into sexual servitude for the remainder of your stay. It is a sad, lowly existence, but if you are unwilling, or unable to defend yourself, that is what you have to look forward to. If you do not make an example of someone, you yourself will become the example.

Chapter 19

The next portion you are about to read was dictated to the author through blinding tears in my eyes and twisted thoughts spinning around inside my head. It was almost as difficult to talk about, as it was to endure. It took every ounce of strength that I could muster to come clean with what I am telling you all now. I fought the author tooth and nail to keep from admitting this. It must have been his rigorous cross-examination that caused me to fold. I am not sure if it was his cold, steely gaze piercing through my lies, or his shockingly sympathetic ear to my story. Whatever it was, it worked, because I broke down and told him every blood curdling detail.

He said to me, "Listen, I know the rules of prison, and I can see it in your eyes. I know what happened to you inside, and you know what happened to you inside. Dig down deep and find courage to tell the world so that people can see karmic justice firsthand. Then and only then, will they forgive you. You have paid more than your penance owed, John. You have experienced true suffering; now you need to forgive yourself, before the world will do so."

I had really hoped that this next portion would be taken to the grave with me, but then this book would not contain the full disclosure of what has happened in my life. What is most important now is honesty, forgiveness, and redemption, because without it, what is the fucking point? I have done both right and wrong, now I choose to do right. I will tell the world every detail of what happened to me.

When I was first incarcerated, I was a naïve, trusting soul. I was immediately targeted due to my name, and the guards hated my notoriety. Please understand that I am in no way placing myself in the ranks of real celebrities. I am referring to the fact that when I was brought into jail there were news cameras and reporters on the scene. Everyone was making a big deal about the fact that I was once again in trouble with the law. A regular person would not have had all of the fanfare and hoopla, but because such a big deal was made, that caused everyone in jail to stand up and take notice of me. Both the guards and inmates despised me for it, and a deal was quickly struck between them to punish me. It was just like every prison film that you have ever seen, only it was real, it was my life.

At first the black inmates started catcalling and

yelling different threats at me.

"New meat!"

"You're dead Bobbitt when the lights go out…"

"I'm gonna make you my bitch cracker."

"Hey sweetie, I'm gonna pump brown sugar in your ass!"

I tried to keep my head down and ignore it. You see, no one gave me a crash course in prison 101, like I just gave you in the previous chapter. If they had, then I would have walked over to the first motherfucker to talk shit to me, and made a fucking example by stomping him until the guards sprayed mace all over the whole fucking place! My first mistake was trying to ignore them. Unbeknownst to me, that showed weakness. Animals love to prey on the weak, and they love it even more when it is ten on one!

My fate was immediately sealed after I let the first person get away with running their mouth. The gang of black inmates knew right then that I was easy pickings. I saw the guards talking with the black guys, but I just figured that was how shit went on in lockdown. Boy was I ever wrong.

In prison slang, "They formulated an intricate plot, to get me alone, so I could get got!"

That is what they were talking about. Everyone wanted to see me suffer, and so they all banded together to make it a reality. What you the reader need to realize is that all of this scheming went on behind the scenes of what the naïve eye could see. I did not know at the time that the goings on was a plan to punish me. If I did, do not think that I would have made it so easy for them. I was simply following the orders given by the guards, and trying to ignore the threats being levied against me. It is that simple folks. I was just trying to get by. I am sure most of you can understand that. I just wish I was better prepared for life on the inside. That is why I have included the basic guidelines to surviving prison in the previous chapter. Just in case any of you ever find yourselves in the precarious situation of being in prison, you will be much better prepared than I was, and hopefully, what happened to me, will never happen to you.

"Bobbitt... shower time! Follow that guard to get a new jumpsuit, soap, and a towel. Don't come back until you're clean superstar!" Yelled the head guard.

I should have known right then that trouble was afoot. I just thought that this blatant hatred of me was because I was an inmate. I did not know he loathed me so utterly and completely that he would mastermind my assault. Prison is an ugly place. The things that you end up seeing, can never be unseen, and if you are not careful the things that can happen, will leave you, forever scarred.

I followed the guard as instructed out of the block and down a hollow, echoing hallway. The fluorescent lights hummed incessantly overhead, as the sound of our footsteps reverberated off of the walls around us. The clickity-clack of the guard's military boots was loud on the hard concrete floor as he led me toward the showers. As we turned the corner toward the shower room, the guard grabbed a small bar of soap off of a shelf and tossed it to me.

"Go strip down and shower. You will have a jumpsuit and towel here when you're finished. Enjoy," he said with a smug smirk upon his unshaven stubbly face. Then he turned and headed back in the opposite direction, down the hall, snickering as he walked away.

Nervously, I stood there for a moment, then I walked through the opening into a small changing area and stripped naked. The air was palpable as it hovered around me with the foul stench of mildew. A damp and dreary sense encompassed me chilling my flesh. I let out a shiver. I felt more than just alone as a twinge of decay permeated my nostrils.

I stepped into the shower room and turned on the closest nozzle as it made a loud creak. The piercing sound of vibrating pipes behind the wall rang out with a loud rumble. I felt the floor shake beneath my feet as I put my hand under the drizzling stream waiting for the water to heat up. I stood there alone pondering the events that had brought me to this place. I hated my life, my existence, and most importantly… my surroundings.

Then, without warning I felt a thunderous crash to the back of my head! For a brief instant I lost consciousness; everything went gray. All conception of time and place was lost. I wallowed in limbo, foggy and confused, as I attempted to regain my composure. Finally, after an undetermined amount of time, I was able to grasp some semblance of reality, only to realize that I was within the clutches of several men, face down on the shower room floor. Black feet were all around me as I struggled with all of my might to be set free. Each of my arms was held tightly by different individuals. My ankles were stretched out forcefully to each side, so that I lay spread eagle on the wet shower room floor. Laughs and taunts ricocheted off of the walls as I felt the blade of a shank pressed tightly against my throat. The metallic taste of blood filled my mouth as the disgusting smell of a man's hot breath filled my nose.

He spoke defiantly into my ear, "You're about to have a train run on your ass by the black evil muthafucker. I hope you fight it too, that'll just make it better!" He let out a sinister laugh, "We've all been wondering which one of the ten of us has the biggest dick? We want you to be the judge."

As he said those last words he shoved every inch of his mammoth cock deep inside my anal cavity! With the initial violation of his penetration I was brought back to the place in my childhood where I was raped. I felt the old familiar sting of my asshole ripping in two. I attempted to retreat into a place in my mind where I had been so long ago. I tried with every fiber of my being to disassociate myself from the torment I was enduring, but to no avail. His angry sodomy kept reining me back into reality. The constant pumping kept ripping and tearing my insides apart.

I screamed out at the top of my lungs but they all just laughed and cheered. The low guttural moans of agony echoed off of the moist walls around us. My miserable cries filled the rank air as turns were taken and shame was handed down. The deepest recesses of my body were violated by one after the next. The crowd jeered as each one took his despicable turn and rammed savagely inside of me. Deeper and deeper, the never ending nightmare continued. With each pelvic thrust, lightning-like flashes blinded my eyes. The pain was excruciating! Even in my youth I did not remember such a sting when my tiny body was violated. The torture seemed to last an eternity. They took their sick and twisted turns, one after the next, as each perpetrator penetrated my soul. Wanton lust was on tap fulfilling all of their shameful desires.

Due to the insanity of the violent assault, I eventually lost consciousness. I awoke sometime later in the infirmary, bloody, bandaged, and unable to move. As I lay there teetering between life and death, face down on a hospital bed, I was able to do some serious soul searching. Staring down at the same pillow over the next few days, (due to the multitudes of stitches holding my asshole together) tears streamed down my face. It took about a week until I finally realized that karma had been served up to me courtesy of hard black inmate dick. How's that for an interesting paradox?

Also, I just wouldn't feel right if I failed to mention that winner of, 'The Biggest Dick Contest' held in my ass, was won by Terrell Washington Jackson III of D-block. He won with a combination of both length and girth, but most of all the deciding factor was the aggression on which he used to deliver his rape. Kudos Terrell… I couldn't sit right for nearly a month.

Chapter 20

Jail, prison, lockup, lockdown, locked all the way the fuck around. Call it whatever you like, no matter the name, it all sucks! Sometimes in life you need something extreme to arise and change the detrimental path you are on. This is what my stint in lockdown did for me.

Don't concern yourself with things that don't concern you, is the number one key to survival. If people would concern themselves less with other people's happiness in life, they might actually be able to find a bit of their own. That is just good planning no matter what piece of real estate you happen to find your feet standing upon. This is something I learned firsthand.

I spent the next few weeks segregated from the rest of the prison population in the infirmary for my own protection. It was in these solemn moments that I truly realized all of the wrong that I had done to Lorena, and I accepted my fate. Truthfully what was I going to do? The only real revenge I could have sought would had involved murder, and I was not willing to cross that line. I had no other alternative than to just take it... literally.

My life and everything in it was ugly for the next few years, but there was one positive, I had learned my lesson. Sure I had to deal with the occasional rape, but what does not kill you makes you stronger… right? There are certain things in life that no matter who you are, you just have to deal with: the inevitability of death, and the consequences of your actions following you wherever you go, are two of them. Karma is a motherfucker. My payback came courtesy of angry guards and inmate cocks. Let me just say… I sure could have done without the latter.

My time in prison consisted of me dodging dicks from the sodomites and being sent around to different branches of the Nevada Department of Corrections. Every time I got acclimated I was moved to a new facility. Everywhere, I was tested simply because my name was John Wayne Bobbitt, and also, because of my abuse charges against Lorena. So I fought often, and I fought hard. Sometimes I won, and sometimes I lost. This was the tragedy that I endured living with a rape-o tag that followed me through the penal system. Things sucked big time in prison, but I can proudly say that I never did. As I have learned, without sacrifice in life there can be no reward.

I managed to survive (though my asshole had been grossly tampered with) until my full sentence had been served. I was cycled back down through the system for release until my feet stood in the same spot where I first came in. I was put right back into the same block, with the same guards, and all of the same inmates where my hell began. The catcalls started up immediately. With only days left until my release I just needed to blend. I could not risk catching another charge. I just wanted to go home, but, they would make sure, that I left with a limp.

I tried to lay low and stay out of sight; nonetheless, they arrived at the entryway of my cell. There I was, cowered in the corner, when I looked up to see five of the nastiest black savage motherfuckers you have ever seen stepping in. They packed themselves into the tight confinement of my cell and the frightful stench of violence followed them in.

The first one spoke, "We wanted to say adios Bobbitt. In fact, we each want to say it twice! If you think it's tight in this cell right now, wait until we all pile into

173

your ass!"

Once the words were uttered, they attacked me. I was beaten to a savage pulp and fucked into a bloody, beaten mess, but that's how it goes sometimes. I received a first rate bon voyage rape from some of the worst kind of people on earth. They hurt me badly… and that is all I have to say about that. If having my cock cut off did not bring me back to even, I am pretty fucking sure the rapes did.

Looking back over the last twenty years, I now recognize that my vicious cycle of abuse has run its course. The savagery with which I used to torment Lorena has been paid back in full. I never set out to be the monster I became, it just happened. It snuck up on me incrementally: gradually over time my misdeeds grew, from shame on me, to downright atrocity. For this I am eternally sorry.

What everyone on the planet needs to realize is that we all need to be thankful for the positive things in our life; everyone has at least something. Forget about the things which are bad because we all have too many. It takes until you have been on this earth for several years to realize that to harbor ill will toward those who wronged you takes too much energy. Life is far too short to worry about things that went wrong. Focus on the things that went right and that will put wind in your sail.

Once again, I need to point out that since I have been given this grandiose stage from which to liberate my conscience my life has been transformed into a wonderful journey.

"The truth shall set you free," is so completely and utterly true that you should all follow this philosophy.

Clarity of mind is priceless metaphorically speaking of course, because there actually is a price to achieve it. The price is simply to accept the consequences of your actions. If you can do that you will then be able to walk through life with a magnanimous heart and the confidence of a righteous person.

Lying, cheating, and stealing, are tools of the weak used for the purpose of deception. Once you eliminate your need to deceive people, everything else falls into place. If you want to achieve bliss, forget about what others want you to do and go after what you really crave. Once you are true to yourself, a beautiful part of life begins.

Society is far too concerned with permissions and conditions of what they are allowed to do. Instead, people should sidestep conformity and create something beautifully original out of sheer ingenuity.

King Solomon (the wisest man who ever lived) said, "All is done for vanity."

Well if that be the case, I challenge you to do something that isn't. Try and do something that is 100% for the betterment of others. There are a few things that I have learned and I am willing to share them in the hopes of helping people to learn from my mistakes.

Life is about finding your center. It is about finding comfort and solace in every situation that you put yourself in. Yes, I said that you put yourself in. I am not saying that unexpected circumstances do not arise in life because they do, but for the most part it is your decisions that led you to where you are. A series of poor decisions will result in a catastrophe at the end. Trust me… I know this all too well.

"Why is this happening to me?"

If you ask that question, you are an idiot, because it is your choices that have put you where you are. "You made your bed so lie in it."

As you know, I have made many decisions in my life both good and bad, but with age comes wisdom, and with wisdom comes discernment, and with discernment comes better decisions. I am sure you have heard the saying, "You are your own worst enemy."

Everyone who makes poor decisions has something that is the rudimentary cause behind their choices. Once you single out, 'your own worst enemy,' you can start truly fixing yourself. If a car has bad breaks, you do not buy new windshield wipers do you? You need to make the appropriate repairs to correct a problem, and it is called a problem because it is difficult to fix. Nothing worthwhile is easy, everything that is worth anything, takes work.

For example, some people say that alcoholics and drug addicts have a disease. I cannot agree with that because a disease is something you do not choose. Sure, I can agree that some people are more genetically predisposed to addiction than others, but I am pretty certain no one wakes up in the morning and says, "Hey, I think I'll get cancer today." Alcoholics and drug addicts choose to continue their detrimental behavior. It is the same scenario with spousal abuse, those of us who abuse, chose this path, now it is up to us to stop the violence. Remember this is coming from a man who beat his wife until she chopped of his cock, so I consider myself to be the king of poor choices.

Everyone has sick and twisted thoughts pop into their heads periodically, but it is the mark of a sane man who is able to control them. When your wants and desires control your decisions, you have failed in life. Take it from me, if it has to be done in secret, it is wrong and you know it. Everyone has a moral compass guiding them through life, make sure yours isn't broken!

In my life I have seen everything from the pits of hell to the highest of mountain peaks. People always ask me, don't you regret some of the things that you have done? To that I say this, I wish some things had not happened, but I do not have the luxury of regretting the things that created the man that I am today. Some of the worst situations have had the greatest impact on my life. I will point out that terrible circumstances create amazing individuals. I have come to grips with what has transpired in my life.

If you want the world to be a better place you need to do something about it. Set precedence by spearheading the movement that makes the change that you want to see implemented. I wanted to put an end to spousal abuse. That is why I came clean after all of these years: in the hopes of helping others understand what made me abuse. It was very difficult to admit my flaws publicly, but if you're not going to help create the solution, then you are part of the problem.

To literally lose your mind and then to be blessed with the ability to openly speak of the experience is a gift that I am proud to share. Through blind omission, my soul gains peace and amazing things begin to happen. Always remember if it was easy to obtain, the reward will be minimal.

If I was granted a single wish, I would ask that my crimes against Lorena never happened, but there are no magical wishes and crimes did happen. I now have the courage to admit and face what I have done, for I am a new man who has learned from his wrongs. In my new life, do you know what I have come to realize? Now that I have finally worked up the courage to tell the truth to the world, I'm sure most people will not forgive me. It is just easier for the haters to keep hating, so that the world can keep on turning. I have poured my heart and soul out onto these pages. I have admitted all of my crimes with zero regard for how it makes me look. How many people in the world can say that?

Yes, I raped and beat my wife, and yes, I too was raped and beaten. I do not offer that as an excuse in any way. Rather, I have learned from it, and now my conscience is clear. Do with it what you wish. As the cold winds of shame continue to blow through and remind me of all that I have done, I will always be, *FOREVER SCARRED*.

11/1/12

I, JOHN WAYNE BOBBITT, HAVE READ 'FOREVER SCARRED' THE JOHN WAYNE BOBBITT STORY AND AGREE WITH, ALL OF THE STORIES, TALES AND ACCOUNTS TOLD WITHIN ITS PAGES.

ALL OF THE FACTS I TOLD TO THE AUTHOR WERE TO THE BEST OF MY RECOLLECTION.

John Wayne Bobbitt
11/01/2012

(Signed statement from John Wayne Bobbitt)

> FRIDAY OCTOBER 5TH, 2012
> IN OFFICE AT LUANNE'S
> HOUSE.
>
> "I FORCED LORENA TO HAVE ANAL SEX."
>
> "I WAS THE WORST HUSBAND THERE EVER WAS."
>
> *John Wayne Bobbitt*
> *Chet Kudela*

(Signed statement from John Wayne Bobbitt)

WED. 11/14/12

BECAUSE OF MY NAME JOHN WAYNE BOBBITT AND MY CHARGES OF ABUSE AGAINST LORENA, THE GUARDS TOLD A GROUP OF BLACK INMATES TO GET ME. THEY GOT ME LATER IN THE SHOWER AND KNOCKED ME OUT. THEY TOOK TURNS ON ME SEXUALLY WITH A SHANK AGAINST MY THROAT. AFTER MY BRUTAL RAPE THE PRISON WAS FORCED TO MOVE ME TO SAFER QUARTERS.

John Wayne Bobbitt

<u>(Signed statement from John Wayne Bobbitt)</u>

Author's notes

Only out of epic tragedy does the opportunity to triumph present itself. In order to write about life you must have lived it to the fullest. I have most certainly done that. Since life itself is the ultimate experience, you must savor every detail of the successes and suffer through all of its failures to have learned enough knowledge to tell a substantial tale. Otherwise who gives a fuck what you have to say?

When it comes to this book, these words are mine and all of the names have been changed. I spoke for John in the first person because he was incapable of speaking for himself. It was a difficult task, but I did the best that I could. I poured myself onto these pages with him. I felt his torment, and experienced his pain. That is the talent of transference. I made it so I was him, and he is me. That was the power this project gave to me.

The reason I write is twofold. Number one, I'm awesome at it, (not bad for a high school dropout either) and number two, is that I love to take a reader on an unexpected journey that evokes multiple emotions and leaves them wiser in the end. I enjoy both entertaining people and teaching them life lessons that I have learned in my travels. This makes me happy, and when done properly, the reader is richer from the experience.

Sometimes as a writer, you become trapped inside certain views. Your talent is shown when you step outside of yourself and give the full view of situations that you are describing. I want the reader to not only read the story, but live it as well. In my attempt to do this, in FOREVER SCARRED The John Wayne Bobbitt Story, I ran into a roadblock, and its name was John Wayne Bobbitt.

Before I tell you about my experience in writing this book first let me tell you a little bit about me. Most people in my hometown think that I am a know it all. Do you know want to know why they think that? Well, first of all, because I know it all, and secondly, because I speak the truth. Anytime, anywhere, I say whatever's on my mind, and it doesn't matter what company I happen to be keeping either. I call a spade, a spade. I see things for what they are, and I call bullshit when I see it. It's that simple. I'm not going to sugarcoat shit for the world so that it's easier for them to swallow. Quite the contrary actually… I hope they choke on the truth, straight out of my motherfucking mouth. Some people say I'm cocky, I say that I'm confident. It's not that I'm arrogant... it's that I'm a dick... there's a difference. It is all just a matter of perspective I suppose.

Sure there are things in this world that I do not know, but that is only because I have not discovered the need to learn them yet. So yes, I am a know it all, and damn proud of it, because, all that I know, I have lived.

So when this project ended up in my lap, I knew that I had to get the story, behind the story, and bring that shit to light. You know, knock it out of the park! I mean really, a big mouthed, know it all like me, placed atop the most grandiose platform from which to speak. Not to mention, like everyone else in the world that followed the tragic events of June 23, 1993, I just wanted to know what went on. I still remember feeling terrible for this guy all the way back when it happened.

What could he have possibly done to make her chop off his cock?

This shit was crazy, but, before we get into all of

that, let me tell you how this project all came about.

      I am a rebel who has never conceded my beliefs since day one. I don't conform to societal norms. I have done it all my way, and I owe no one but the Lord above for where I am today. I left home at a young age in bare feet, in my underwear, with a smashed in face that my father gave me on my way out the door, and I've been rolling on ever since. It was difficult as you can imagine, growing up out in the cruel world alone, but I will spare you a lengthy dissertation (if you want the details then you'll have to read my other novels). Let me break my life down to you in one sentence. I have been both literally and figuratively ass fucked by the world, so I know a thing or two about loss.

      Facing the world alone, I took to selling drugs as a means to survive. Through some clever tutelage from a 'streetwise professor,' I garnered a plethora of useful knowledge to subsist. Along with my newfound wisdom came a voracious drug habit that haunted me as it continued to escalate over the years. Finally, it all culminated in multiple arrests, near death experiences, and a year-long stint in lock up. Having always written, but never taken it seriously, I began to hone my skills for prose, after just a few weeks inside. I found that I needed a new hobby instead of fighting with the other inmates. Turns out the black guys didn't think I was as entertaining as I did. After ending up in solitary confinement I decided I would try reading some books to help pass the time. What happened next was a life changing experience on several levels.

I was roughly three weeks into a 365 day sentence when I found myself granted (due to my newly acquired isolation situation) with both the time and the want to read. At this point in my life, I was 36 years old, and I had read only four books in my life, and one of them was The Bible. The first book I tackled was THE CATCHER IN THE RYE by J.D. Salinger. Well, let me just say this, I read it twice because I thought I was actually missing pages from the book. I thought it was boring, long winded, and just never really went anywhere. Teen angst my ass! More like lame ass dribble. To be totally honest I felt that my comprehension must be lacking because I couldn't understand what all the fuss was about. There was zero shock, awe, or even a twinge of excitement. I am not going to sit here and blast such an acclaimed literary work anymore than this, to me, I just didn't get the point…

enough said.

The next great American novel that I read was, THE PEARL, by John Steinbeck. While I thought the story was good, but not great either, just good, I felt robbed to find out that the moral was that money corrupts people. Really, eighty-nine pages to tell me that? I had already known that, actually I learned that shit years ago. I could have told you that in a paragraph, and had you laughing the whole time. I never even cracked a smile reading that entire book. So I whipped both of the books out of my cell, smoked a fat ass joint, and thought to myself, "I'm going to write a better book than all of the bullshit, long winded, boring novels filling the world's bookshelves!"

I have always known that my existence was one of importance, even though the universe can make you feel rather insignificant at times, especially when you're pondering life, death, and fate, from the inside of a jail cell. Yet, I was convinced I could do a better job. In all honesty, I am a superficial, arrogant, yet incredibly insecure asshole, who needs constant accolades from my minions to prove my own self-worth… but hey, at least I can admit my flaws. What's your excuse?

Then, out of sheer spite I defiantly picked up my pen and boldly placed my note book in front of me. I wanted to sound really intelligent too, so that I could show the world just how smart I was. I thought for a moment and just began to write the thoughts that were in my head. I studied the first sentence for a moment and thought to myself, "Hey, that sounds pretty good." Then I wrote another sentence and studied it. Well that sounded good too, and pretty soon I had a paragraph. Shortly after that I had an entire page and by the time lights out came that night, I had my first chapter.

Over the next couple of months I spent my time drinking freeze-dried Colombian coffee, smoking pot, (that at one time, very recently, was stuffed up someone's asshole before getting to me) and writing a book. After I wrote the second chapter, I knew I would create something special. It was this first novel that landed me the opportunity to work on John Wayne Bobbitt's story.

When J.W.B wanted to do his story, someone he knew who had just read my first novel said, "Hey John, you need to get this Christopher Mark Kudela guy to write your book. I just finished his novel, THEY CALL ME KRUD, and this guy can make even the worst person look good."

So his people contacted my people, and the rest, as they say, is history.

I have been told (on more than one occasion mind you) that the Chris Kudela philosophy only works for one person… Chris Kudela. I have also been told that I am indeed a text book narcissist. Well, as I tell everyone who questions my way of thinking, "If your world doesn't revolve around you, that's your first problem. Your second is that most likely you're an asshole."

You can only truly be happy, when you're living out your dreams. And you can only be truly free, when you have nothing left to lose. True success is measured by being able to do what you want too, whenever you want to do it. Some people have no clue what they want, and that is why they will never know happiness. Other people know exactly what they want, but have no clue how to get it. Happiness is not a thing you hold in your hand… it's a state of mind. Once you realize that, you can achieve it. Happiness is obtainable, but only when you start being honest with yourself. You must embrace the real you, and love you for what you are, and don't pass judgment on others; then no one can pass judgment on you. "Free your mind, your ass will follow."

I'm the kind of guy who has seen cash in stacks, but I have also lied in the gutter without a penny in my pocket. I have been locked in a cell, but I have also gazed off of my penthouse balcony more times than I care to reminisce. I have been kicked out of every school that I had ever attended and evicted from every home that I have ever lived in. I have also been fired from every job that I have ever held, so by all conventional forms of measure, I am a loser. If you were to judge a whale on his ability to breathe fire or live on land, then by that standard he would be a failure. But if you were to judge him on his ability to hold his breath and dive to the depths of the ocean, then he would be a winner. So by that rationale, since I am the happiest person that I know, I am the ultimate winner. Oh, touché my nautical friend.

Now with all of that being said, let me tell you of the seesaw battle that was involved bringing this project to fruition. When I agreed to tell this incredible tale of woe I knew it would be difficult to uncover the truth from the deepest recesses of shame where it was buried. The day that I first met John Wayne Bobbitt, I knew I didn't like him. He was an obtuse, scatterbrain, who was all over the board with a photo album of porno chicks under his arm. I thought to myself, is this clown for real? Though I thought it was odd, our meeting in no way prepared me for the literal roller coaster that I would be riding.

After agreeing to take on the project, we sat down for a little Q & A. One careful lie after the next was woven into a twisted web of deceit, and it would be hard to uncover the truth. J.W.B's lies had all been fabricated over years, then reworked and tweaked to fit every scenario. In the beginning after a bit of research, I was sold on his innocence. Lorena's first statement to the police did that for me.

"He always have orgasm, he doesn't wait for me to orgasm, he's a greedy lover." She said in her broken Ecuadorian accent to the first investigator to question her. Those words, well to me anyway, didn't fit the later allegations of rape. Her defense seemed contrived by a jaded woman, and a man-hating legal defense.

So after J.W.B's profession that he was, in fact, the victim, it all seemed plausible. I was convinced that I could blast holes in Lorena's case and pen his way to a publicly perceived acceptance of innocence. My grandiose vision was perpetuated by J.W.B's cleverly contrived falsities, coupled with the amount of alcohol that I consumed at our first meeting.

I mean really, after twenty years, why would he lie? So I went home and hit the ground running. I wrote five chapters of scintillating prose defending my newly acquired subject in just as many days. I had this shit on lockdown!

It wasn't until we met again, (when I was sober) that I looked into J.W.B's eyes and saw a man full of guilt standing on a platform of lies. Truth be told, I was clearly smitten by the idea of this project and I wanted to believe him. But immediately upon this discovery I posed to him the ultimatum, I write the truth, or I write nothing at all. It took over four hours, and a collection of harsh words, but he finally agreed.

Over the next several months we met at least once a week in grueling interview sessions that at times spiraled out of control. On Monday he said one thing, and by Wednesday it was completely different. Anger toward his duplicity began to get the better of me. I began to truly despise my subject. I won't say it was maddening, but I will say I was getting pretty fucking annoyed.

He would, after an hour of interrogation, admit what he did to Lorena. Then a day or so later, he would say that he didn't do what he said that he did the day before. It was exhausting. I think in all actuality it would be hard for anyone to come clean on all that J.W.B did.

Like someone told me when all of this was taking place, "Chris, people aren't like you. No one can just openly admit to all of the wrong that they have done like you do."

To which I replied, "Well they should, because it's the only way to truly be forgiven."

In my heart I believe that J.W.B will always care too much of what the public perception of him is, but it took great courage to finally admit the truth, even though he has attempted to recant it now. I was also smart enough to cover my ass and make him sign papers each time he admitted something big. I had to because he would change his mind whenever he felt people would laugh or mock him. He was wildly concerned that people would accuse him of being gay because he was raped in prison. Guys in prison believe only the guy getting fucked is gay.

"I'm not gay he sucked my dick, or, I'm not gay, I fucked him."

I have heard those words many times. That is the common, uneducated, misconceptions of foolish people in jail. Like I explained to him, no one can fault a man for being raped by ten men, and anyone who does, is an idiot anyway, so who cares what he has to say. But those are my beliefs, Christopher Mark Kudela, I could never get John Wayne Bobbitt to see the light.

It was conversations like this that infuriated me daily. I am not trying to bash my subject I am just trying to point out the daunting task that went into facilitating this project. If it wasn't for the publisher at the time, (who later recused himself after J.W.B. threatened to have me killed if this book was published) talking me down off of the ledge, on more than one occasion, this book would have never reached completion. I was going to quit and throw in the towel at least ten times, but he (the publisher) would reign me back in. He is a genius negotiator and a brilliant man that's for sure, because without him, this would have never happened.

Let me give you an example of J.W.B's behavior driving me nuts in some actual dialog from an interview session. I was interviewing him about his marriage to Lorena and I needed specifics. I was looking to write about the abuse that had taken place between them and I wanted the gritty details. You know the hardcore sick shit, i.e. the ass fucking her on the kitchen floor that he later described, but at first he told me this:

"John, what's the absolute worst thing that you did to Lorena in your four years of marriage?"

Somewhat perplexed, he responded, "The absolute worst?"

"Yeah, the one thing that resonates in your brain that you wish you had never done to her. The one thing that she'll never forget, that one thing that she could never forgive, or that she'll never be able to get over. The one thing, twenty years later, that still keeps her up at night hating your ass."

I pleaded for something, anything, one of his many skeletons from deep within his darkened closet of secrets. I hung on bated breath, full of anticipation for his response. I was seated on the edge of my office chair (literally), with my pen in hand, pressed to my legal pad, ready to write this terrible deed.

When he responded, "The worst thing that I ever did was I ignored her. That was the worst thing, because women hate being ignored."

I just about shit myself from both laughter and shock. "No John! Do you know what women really hate?"

"What?"

"Getting their ass kicked and being repeatedly raped like that you have already told me that you did to her! That is what women really hate you asshole!"

"Well they hate being ignored too."

"Well let me break this down to you another way."

I wanted to yank my fucking hair out. As he continued to spout some useless babble about whatever-the-fuck-ever, I walked out from behind my desk with my coffee cup in hand. I sauntered across the room as he continued rambling until I was right beside him.

"I'm sorry John, were you saying something?"

To which he responded, "Didn't you listen to me?"

"No, I ignored you. Did that hurt your feelings?"

"Not really."

"Good. Now imagine I beat you up, flipped you over, ripped off your pants, and then ass fucked the shit out of you. Screaming the whole time, look what you made me do! Look what you made me do! Now which do you think would be worse?"

I must point out that this was a month or so before J.W.B's admission of being raped in prison, so I wasn't trying to be mean, I was just proving a point. The point being by the way, that while women don't like being ignored, they will eventually cut your cock off for being repeatedly sodomized. It worked too, because he not only saw the point, he later admitted to the rape with tears in his eyes. I will say that my hatred of him dissipated when he did and I gained a newfound respect for him. It's not easy to admit the horrible secrets that we all shamefully hide from the world. It takes a big man to do so (though once again I must point out he now claims none of this happened, even though there are several signed statements to the contrary).

Just a little FYI for those interested out there, this is something I learned years ago. When you question someone about something that they don't necessarily want to admit, you need to become a student of the pantomime. You need to study every gesture and movement, watching closely for any inconsistency that may arise. This will tell you what your subject is attempting to hide.

Very few people have the ability to tell believable lies. There is almost always an enormous loophole that is so abundantly clear even a blind man could see it. That is how it was when J.W.B and I discussed his prison stint, and subsequent rapes. He had information that I wanted, but he was unwilling to give it. My trump card was that I knew from being locked-up, because of his celebrity status and abuse charges, that sodomy was a forgone conclusion the moment he stepped through the gates of confinement.

There is no bigger trophy to inmates in prison to than a rape-o with a celebrity name attached to him. So it had to of happened. I'm not Nostradamus, I just understand the rules. One thing you can always count on in jail is that criminals are going to be criminals, and rapists get raped. That's just how it goes on the inside.

Truthfully, I am sure that J.W.B has wanted to get that off of his chest for a long time, he just couldn't. I suppose the people who have surrounded him in his life, before knowing me that is, wouldn't have had a sympathetic ear to his sodomy. As for me on the other hand I did, and I hope that he finally has some peace.

I have told J.W.B that what he needs is to disappear. Ride off into the sunset, change his name, and never step in front of a camera again. But... he is incapable of doing so because he is addicted to the craziness of it all. He is a true product of his environment. He will always attempt (in vain mind you) to prove how smart he is. He is failure in perpetuity. I am sorry for the brutal honesty, but that is the cold grim reality at hand. John Wayne Bobbitt will always fail, because he has been conditioned from birth to do so.

Now for the rest of you out there willing to learn

from his mistakes, I tell you this. If you want to find happiness you need to first forgo all of the foolish wants of your youth, i.e. drugs, drunkenness, fighting for foolish causes, as these will only fill your world with troubles. (I think spousal rape while toping that list, should go without saying.) Secondly, you must surround yourself with likeminded individuals, or abide alone. Otherwise the wants of others will hamper you with foolhardy demands.

I knew after writing the second chapter of my first novel that I had found my niche. After the completion of the last sentence, transcendence occurred. I broke down in tears as I wrote the last line of the book, and from then on I knew exactly what I wanted to do with of my life. The true magnificence of my discovery came later that evening when I went to sleep on the shittiest mattress, in the crappiest place on earth. Yet, I had the best night of sleep that I have ever had. From that day forward, I no longer have had any migraine headaches or nightmares, which have plagued me since my youth. I thank God every day for all of my blessings.

In conclusion, even though you claim you will have me killed for the publication of this book, I kindly thank

John Wayne Bobbitt for the opportunity to tell his story. You drove me nuts, well not literally, but it was an interesting experience. Thanks for the opportunity to showcase my skills.

My most sincere thanks go out to My Ace, Luanne Barber. Without you I would never have become the man that I am today. I would also like to acknowledge the masterful editing and contributions of both Christie Sauer Fifer and Dawn Cenname Fletch. You ladies rock like granite. If there are two finer women in this field, I certainly don't know of them. Cover design by Theresa Lorenti.

And of course most importantly, I thank God above all things, for without you, I am nothing. Thank you for blessing me with the talent to tell tales and the ability to make it through this crazy thing called life. I will do all that you ever ask of me, because you are my Father, and I love you.

To all of the rest out there, I hope that you enjoyed, FOREVER SCARRED.

Sincerely,

Christopher Mark Kudela

Printed in Great Britain
by Amazon